ISBN 978-1-330-20356-9
PIBN 10051866

1 MONTH OF
FREE
READING

at
www.ForgottenBooks.com

By purchasing this book you are eligible for one month membership to ForgottenBooks.com, giving you unlimited access to our entire collection of over 700,000 titles via our web site and mobile apps.

To claim your free month visit:
www.forgottenbooks.com/free51866

English
Français
Deutsche
Italiano
Español
Português

www.forgottenbooks.com

Mythology Photography **Fiction**
Fishing Christianity **Art** Cooking
Essays Buddhism Freemasonry
Medicine **Biology** Music **Ancient
Egypt** Evolution Carpentry Physics
Dance Geology **Mathematics** Fitness
Shakespeare **Folklore** Yoga Marketing
Confidence Immortality Biographies
Poetry **Psychology** Witchcraft
Electronics Chemistry History **Law**
Accounting **Philosophy** Anthropology
Alchemy Drama Quantum Mechanics
Atheism Sexual Health **Ancient History**
Entrepreneurship Languages Sport
Paleontology Needlework Islam
Metaphysics Investment Archaeology
Parenting Statistics Criminology
Motivational

THE

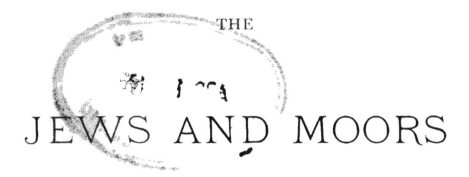

JEWS AND MOORS

IN

SPAIN.

BY

RABBI JOS. KRAUSKOPF.

KANSAS CITY·

M. BERKOWITZ & CO, PUBLISHERS AND PRINTERS

1887.

To

The Members of Congregation

B'NAI JEHUDAH

of

Kansas City, Missouri,

In Deep Appreciation of their Kindness

and Encouragement

This Volume

Is Respectfully Dedicated.

PREFACE.

THIS volume is a reprint of newspaper reports of a series of lectures delivered by the author from the pulpit of Congregation B'nai Jehudah, Kansas City, Mo., during the Fall and Winter of 1885-1886.

The lectures were prepared to fulfill the requirements of popular discourses, and designed to convey information upon a highly important epoch of the world's history, that is almost neglected in English literature.

The thought of publishing these lectures in book form was utterly foreign to the author throughout their preparation, until an urgent solicitation from very many persons, both Jews and Gentiles, in all parts of this country, whose interest in these lectures was aroused by their wide-spread republication by the Press, made it a duty.

Kansas City, Mo., January, 1887.

The following are two of the many letters addressed to the author, requesting him to have his lectures on "THE JEWS AND MOORS IN SPAIN" published in book form.

LETTER FROM HON. T. T. CRITTENDEN,

Ex-Governor of the State of Missouri.

KANSAS CITY, MO., MARCH 29 1886.

RABBI JOSEPH KRAUSKOPF.

DEAR SIR:—Having read with pleasure and edification the series of lectures delivered in the Synagogue, Kansas City, Mo., entitled "THE JEWS AND MOORS IN SPAIN," in which you treat of the social, political, religious and intellectual life of these Oriental nations, may I inquire if it is your purpose to have them published in book form?

I think the lectures too valuable, too full of prolonged historic research and thought to live only one day in the columns of a daily newspaper. Even if they were designed "to adorn a tale or point a moral" of the great race to which you belong, whose history commenced with Abraham and will end with that of the human race, still the history of that race was (and is) so intimately interlaced with the history of the other races for the intervening centuries, that the lectures are in part, so much the history of the other races, that they can be read and studied by all men without prejudice or animosity One thing is certain, you have in the lectures divested history of much of its dry and useless details, and make it a thrilling romance of facts, presented in the simplest and purest Anglo-Saxon language.

I know not how others view the lectures, only speak this for myself—no library is complete without the History of the Jewish race, and no history of that race for the period covered, is more comprehensive, truthful and impartial than that presented in these lectures. I think the book would find a ready sale in all thinking, reading communities.

Very Truly Yours,

THOS. T. CRITTENDEN.

LETTER FROM ARNOLD KREKEL,

Judge of the U. S. Court, Western District of Missouri.

———————

KANSAS CITY, MO, APRIL 2, 1886.

RABBI JOSEPH KRAUSKOPF.

MY DEAR SIR:—Having attended a number of your lectures on "THE HISTORY OF THE JEWS AND MOORS IN SPAIN," and read such as I did not hear, allow me to give expression to my views regarding the same. Aside from the interest the student of history must always feel in that part of history of which your lectures treat, the manner of treatment specially interested me. Relating historical facts, too often becomes dry and irksome, and it requires more than ordinary skill of presentation to make the subject interesting and attractive. In this you have fully succeeded by interweaving with the facts those matters which enliven the picture. A knowledge of the social condition of a people, and the relation to which they stand to their age, enables us to judge of their worth and the influence they exercised. Your lectures, as a whole, presented a life-breathing social picture of the times and people, and as the civilization of Europe was largely effected by the Jews and Moors, their history embraces to a large extent the history of civilization, and thereby acquires an interest not limited to the people and countries of which your lectures give so interesting an account. A publication in permanent form of your lectures would advance our knowledge of that part of history to which we have always looked for instruction and guidance, and I hope you may find a way of accomplishing this object.

Very Respectfully,

A. KREKEL.

THE JOURNAL published yesterday morning the eighteenth
and last of the series of lectures delivered by Rabbi Krauskopf on "THE JEW AND MOOR IN SPAIN." From first to last
these lectures have been of absorbing interest. The Synagogue has been crowded on the occasion of their delivery,
and it was with regret that the Rabbi's hearers heard that
the lecture on Friday night was the last of the series.

It is the purpose of Rabbi Krauskopf to have his
lectures issued in book form. They will make an attractive
volume, and will no doubt be widely read. Rabbi Krauskopf is a graphic writer, and his lectures upon "THE JEW AND
MOOR IN SPAIN" are a series of historical occurrences related in a manner that serves to chain the reader's attention—old world scenes are accurately and vividly described. The reader is taken through all the struggles,
the defeats and the triumphs of the Jews. Their arts, their
industry, their upright dealings and their steadfast adherence
to their religion through trials and persecutions are related
with a proud belief that they were God's chosen people,
working out their destiny according to His will. The
lecturer started with the Jews as he found them, a prosperous
community in southwestern Europe, busily engaged in transforming Spain into a granery and garden spot of Europe,
respected by their heathen neighbors, happy and contented.
He passed on to the period of persecution in the Sixth
Century when Christianity of a somewhat forcible nature
attempted the conversion of the Jews by persecution; when
many were massacred and others driven into exile. Then
came the Arab invasion and during the period of Moham-

medan supremacy the Jews were again allowed to live in peace and the exercise of their own religious rites. For eight centuries the Jews and the Moors worked side by side and the once down-trodden people rose to affluence and high position.

With the decline of Mohammedan power, and the expulsion of the Moors by the Spaniards, the Jews were again reduced to a pitiable state. Spain arose to enormous power, but that, too, has waned, and the population of 30,000,000 people has dwindled to about half that number. The manufactures, the commerce and the agricultural, the universal prosperity which the Jews had built up disappeared, and the glory of Spain departed as rapidly as it had been acquired. In the expulsion of the Jews and Moors alone does Rabbi Krauskopf attribute the ruin of Spain.

The lectures read like a romance. They are an historical romance, told in a charming manner, full of descriptions accurate, truthful. When they are compiled the volume will undoubtedly meet with a large sale. It was not the original intention of the Rabbi to issue his lectures in book form, but many people, both Jews and Chrstians, have requested him verbally and by letter to do so, and he has decided to grant their requests.

CONTENTS OF CHAPTERS.

CONTENTS.

CHAPTER III.

CHAPTER IV.

CHAPTER V.

CHAPTER XI.

Marvelous Intellectual Superiority of Moors and Jews
..Moors Excel the Jews in the Sciences
They Introduce the Mathematical Sciences. Their
Progress in Astronomy. Absurd Refutations by the
Christian Clergy. The Researches into Chemistry.
Zoology and Geology .They Anticipate Modern Dis
coveries. Europe's Ingratitude.

CHAPTER XII.

Spain's Prosperity Stimulates Literature Lavish Pro-
visions for Education. Caliphs Patrons of Learning
Vast Libraries Embodying the Knowledge of the Day
.Poetry Especially Fostered. Story-telling..Jewish
and Moorish Poetry Contrasted. Jehuda Ha Levy
Charisi. Gabirol. Moses Ben Ezra.

CHAPTER XIII.

Alexandria, the Intellectual Metropolis of the World
A Prodigious Stimulus Given to Learning The
Septuagint Development of Grecian Philosophy into

The Jews and Moors in Spain.

CHAPTER I.

A DAY IN CORDOVA.

SIX AND EIGHT AND TEN CENTURIES BACK IN THE WORLD'S HISTORY.
— OUR ENTRANCE INTO SPAIN.—A MIRACLE.—THE BEAUTIFUL
GUADALAQUIVIR.—OUR BRONZE COMPLEXIONED OARS
MAN.—PAIR CORDOVA.—THE CITY OF THE
ARTS AND SCIENCES.—NIGHT.—A SE-
RENADE. —OUR DEPARTURE.

IT is with the past that we shall commune in these pages. Events and scenes, beautiful and loathsome, joyous and tearful, ennobling and degrading, will follow each other in rapid succession. There will be much that, despite the very best of historic sources, and most reliable and impartial authorities, will be accepted as fabulous or will be rejected as incredible or impossible. Achievements will be described, that will startle us for their peerless magnificence and lead us to suppose that we are not dealing with facts, but with the imaginations of some rich phantasy or with the fictitious colorings of a mind enthusiastic for an ideal society; and miseries and sufferings will be depicted that will strike terror into our very soul, and cause our heart to rise in rebellion against the mind, when asked to believe them as actual occurrences, and not as some distressing and revolting and bloodstained work of fiction, written by some hellish fiend for the amusement or for the schooling of the vicious indwellers of the bottomless pit of Tophet.   And yet, it will be history, and true history, strange and incredible, marvelous and anomalous though it may appear.   Six and eight and ten centuries have since passed by, and the most wonderful of all centuries they have been, centuries that chronicle the birth and prodigious growth of the sciences and inventions, the creation and successful continuance of republican and constitutional governments, the breaking down of castes and barriers between man and man, the suppression of political and religious terrorism and these blessed results have so tickled our conceit, have so raised our moral standard that it is almost impossible for us to properly conceive—either in all its grandeur or in all its baseness—that era of the past, which we are about to traverse.

But know we must, and therefore, what the mind refuses to believe, and what the heart refuses to credit, let the eye see.   Let us think ourselves back six and eight and ten centuries. Let us enter upon a far and distant journey. Away we speed.   Far, far across the wild Atlantic.   We have reached the sunny land of Spain. Here let us pause for a hasty inspection.   It will not take us long, for that country, that is among the poorest of all European countries to-day,

whose reeking filth has recently made it a scene
of revelry to the ravashing plague, whose stupendous ignorance, and appalling superstitions,
have made it a by-word among the civilized people of the earth, that country, so backward now,
will certainly have no attractiveness for us, ten
centuries earlier in its history.

Lo! A miracle! The magic wand of some frol-
icksome fay must have suddenly transformed the
land of expected filth and wretchedness into a
beauteous fairyland. Amidst rapturous admiration of the indescribable beauties, which meet our
gaze everywhere, we glide along upon the placid
surface of the Guadalquivir, in which a wondrously
clear blue sky glasses itself, and splendrous
palaces and gorgeous parks are reflected. We
have entered beautiful Andalusia. We glide
along the southern declivity of the Sierra Morena. Suddenly there breaks upon our view a
scene of beauty that mocks every attempt at description. We ask our black eyed, bronze complexioned and proud featured oarsman for the
name of that magnificent city that lies stretched
for miles along the right bank. He understands
us not. We address him in French, in German,
in Greek, in Latin. No answer. We are at
our wits' end. We must know, and so we seek
recourse, as a lost resort, to our mother tongue,
the language of the Hebrews, and his face bright-
ens, and his tongue is loosened, and in accents
as melodious and pure as it must have been spok-
en by David himself, when he sang to his harp,
the words of his own heaven-inspired psalms he

makes reply : "What ye behold, ye strangers, is the city of Cordova, the government seat of the valiant and chivalrous, and scholarly and liberal, and art-loving Caliph Abderrahman III."

We are burning with a desire to see that city, whose simple outlines display such bewildering elegance. With our courteous oarsman as guide, we advance along the street that leads from the river bank. We gaze and gaze in awe-stricken silence. . Amazement is expressed on every countenance. Our eyes are dazzled with the enchanting magnificence that abounds. We have reached the palace of the Caliph. Are we dreaming? Are we under the power of some magic spell? Is this a whim of some sportive, mischief-loving fay? Have we not thought ourselves some ten centuries back? Are we in the midst of the Dark Ages; in European lands, and among the people of the tenth century, concerning whose stupendous ignorance and loathsome filth historians have had so much to say? Has history deceived us in its teaching that the people of Europe, six and eight centuries back had scarcely emerged from the savage state, that they inhabited floorless, chimneyless, windowless huts, those of princes and monarchs differing only in their having rushes on the floor and straw mats against the walls, that they fed on roots and vetches and bark of trees, clothed in garments of untanned skin which remained on the body till they dropped in pieces, that there existed scarcely a city, everywhere pathless forest and howling wastes?

It is not a dream. Neither has history deceived us. We are in European lands, but among Oriental people. We are in the midst of the prime of the dark ages, but we are in the Southern part of Spain, in Andalusia, in the city of Cordova, a city of 200,000 houses, and 1,000,000 inhabitants, of hundreds of parks and public gardens, of menageries of foreign animals, of aviaries of rare birds, of factories in which skilled workmen display their art in textures of silk, cotton, linen, and all the miracles of the loom, in jewelry and in filigree works, in works of art, and in scientific instruments and apparatus. We are in the city that, even then, could boast of a college of music, of libraries, of public schools, of universites in which instructions were given in the sciences and philosophies and languages, and literatures and arts. We are in the city of art and culture and learning, the city made famous and beautiful by the literary and cultured Moors and Jews, whose prosperity continued as long as the followers of Mohammed and the followers of Moses were permitted to dwell in peace side by side, but whose glory vanished as soon as Christianity banished the Jews and Moors from Spain. But we must not indulge in any reflections now. Our raven locked guide, whose beautiful form, and winning countenance, and melodious voice involuntarily remind us of the beautiful lover of the love-inflamed Shulamite in "Solomon's Song," beckons, and we must follow. On we march, and with every step new and matchless beauties unroll themselves before us. We know

not what we shall admire first, and most, whether the polished marble balconies that overhang
luscious orange gardens, or the courts with the
cascades of water beneath the shades of the cypress trees, or the artificial lakes, supplied with
water by hydraulic works, replete with fish;
whether the shady retreats with inlaid floors and
walls of exquisite mosaic, vaulted with stained
glass and speckled with gold, over which streams
of water are continually gushing, or the fountains
of quicksilver, that shoot up in glittering glo-
bules and fall with a tranquil sound like fairy
bells; whether the apartments into which cool
air is drawn from the flower gardens, in summer
by means of ventilating towers and in winter
through earthen pipes or caleducts imbedded in
the walls—the hypocaust, in the vaults below, or
the walls adorned with arabesque and paintings
of agricultural scenes and views of paradise, or
the ceilings corniced with fretted gold, other
great chandeliers with their hundreds and hundreds of lamps; whether the columns of Greek,
Italian, Spanish and African marble, covered with
verd-antique and incrusted with lapis lazuli, or
the furniture of sandal and citron wood, inlaid with mother of pearl, ivory, silver, or re-
lieved with gold and precious malachite, or
the costume of the ladies woven in silk and
gold, and decorated with gems of chrysolites,
hyacinths, emeralds and sapphires ; whether
the vases of rock crystal, Chinese porcelains,
the embroidered Persian carpets with which the
floors are covered, the rich tapestry that hang

along the walls, or the beautiful gardens, profuse with rare and exotic flowers, winding walks, bowers of roses, seats cut out of the rock, crypt-like grottoes hewn into the stone; whether the baths of marble, with hot and cold water, carried thither by pipes of metal, or the niches, with their dripping alcarazzas, or the whispering galleries for the amusement of the women, or the laby-rinths and marble play-courts for the children.

On and on we pass, and new beauties still. We pass mosques and synagogues whose archi-tectural finish is still the admiration and model of the world, and our gentle guide informs us that a public school is attached to each, in which the children of the poor are taught to read and write. We pass academies and universities, and our guide assures us that many a Hebrew pre-sides over the Moorish institutions of learning. He reads the expression of surprise on our coun-tenance, for we think of the striking con-trast between his Mohammedan liberality and the intolerance of the other European countries, from which they are scarcely weaned as yet, and he modestly imforms us that the Mo-hammedan maxim is, that "the real learning of a man is of more importance than any particular religious opinions he may entertain" And as the famous scholars pass in and out, our guide mentions them by name, and speaks of their brilliant accomplishments, of professors of Arabic classical literature, of professors of mathematics and astronomy, compilers of dictionaries similar to those now in use, but of larger copiousness, one

of these covering sixty volumes, he points out
the lexicographers of Greek and Latin and Hebrew and Arabic, and the encyclopedists of the
"Historical Dictionary of Sciences," the poets of
the satires, odes and elegies, and the inventors
of the rhyme, the writers of history, of chronology,
of numismatics, mathematics, astronomy, of pulpit oratory, of agriculture, of topography, of statistics, of physics, philosophy, medicines, dentistry
surgery, zoology, botany, pharmacy, and of the
numerous other branches of learning.

Night has set in.   Men are gathering around
their evening fires to listen to the wandering lit-
erati, who exercise their wonderful powers of
tale telling, and edify the eager listeners by such
narratives as those that have descended to us in
the "Arabian Nights' Entertainments."   The
dulcet strains of the dreamy and love-awaking
mandolin, accompanying the rapturous love song
of some chivalrous knight to his lady fair, break
on our ears.   Soon all is silent.   We fain would
stay, but our guide is weary from his day's task.
Perchance the sweet strains of the serenade have
awakened within his bosom tender longings for
his fair Shulamite, "whose eyes are as the dove's,
and whose lips are like a thread of scarlet, and
whose speech is comely," (Song of Solomon,
chap. iv.) to whom he would eagerly speed.
And so we retrace our steps.   For miles we
walk in a straight line, by the light of public
lamps; seven hundred years after this time
there was not so much as one public lamp in
London.

For miles we walk along solidly paved streets. In Paris centuries subsequently, whoever stepped over his threshold on a rainy day stepped up to his ankles in mud. We have reached the bank of the Guadalquivir, and we have parted with our guide.

We have seen in one day more than we ever dared to dream of; enough to tempt us to visit it again and again, and not only Cordova, but also Grenada, Toledo, Barcelona, Saragossa, Seville, and other cities, to acquire a better acquaintanceship with their scholars and institutions, and with the wondrous advance of their civilization. Before we return, however, we shall visit France, Germany, England and Northern Spain, during the same era of the world's history, about ten centuries back, and the scenes that we shall meet there will enable us to appreciate all the better the benefits which the Moors and the Jews lavished upon Europe, and we shall become the more painfully conscious of the unatonable crime Spain has committed in expelling the Moors from Europe, and degrading the Jews for centuries to the dregs of mankind.

CHAPTER II.

EUROPE DURING THE DARK AGES.

UPON THE OCEAN.—DESOLATE EUROPE.—LONGING AFTER CORDOVA.
SOUTHERN SPAIN CONTRASTED WITH THE REST OF EUROPE.
REVOLTING UNCLEANLINESS.—ASCETIC MONKS ESTABL-
ISH THE BELIEF THAT CLEANLINESS OF BODY
LEADS TO POLLUTION OF SOUL.—IN-
TELLECT FETTERED HAND AND
FOOT.—CLERGY RE-
TARDING PROGRESS.—SECULAR KNOWLEDGE SPURNED.

On, on, we glide upon the smooth, broad bosom of the majestic Guadalquivir, along graceful groves and parks and palaces, through woods and meads, hills and dales, shades and sun. A last glance, and beauteous Cordova hides her proud head behind the sun-kissed horizon.

Fair Cordova, fair Andalusia, fair Southern lands of Spain, fare ye well, take our brief adieu, till we visit you anew.

On, on, we sail, towards the Atlantic now we speed.

We have reached the shores of the interminable ocean. Its wild waves dash fiercely against the rock-ribbed shores, as if impatient for our return. Our goodly ship, staunch and strong, raises and lowers its festooned bow upon the heaving billows of the waters vast, and its pendant is playing in the wind, and its sails from the foreroyal to the mizzenroyal, and up to the very top of the mainroyal are furled to the full, in its heartv welcome to our return. We embark, and—

"On, on the vesse¹ flies, the land is gone.
Four days are sped, but with the fifth, anon,
New shores descried, make every bosom gay,"

For we are to visit beautiful France, and learned Germany, and busy England, and Italy, of classic fame.

Once more we are on the continent. Once more our observations are to be put to the task. Once more we think ourselves some six and eight and ten centuries back in the world's history. Once more the eye is to be made to see what the mind has refused to credit.

Dreary and chilling and appalling are the scenes that now break upon our view. Longingly we think of thee, fair Cordova, thou pride of beauteous Andalusia. We think of thy pavements of marble, of thy fountains of jasper, of thy wondrous artistic skill, of thy exquisite gardens, of thy famous poets and musicians, artists and writers, philosophers and scientists, of thy chivalrous knights and enchanting ladies. Longingly we think of thy wondrous beauty, that would, indeed, in our present surroundings, have sounded fabulous had not our own eyes seen it. Had

we been suddenly transplanted from the midst of
blossoming and ripening summer, joyous because
of its balmy breath and the melodious song of its
birds, and the fragrant breath of its flowers, and
the gladdening sight of its ripening fruit into the
midst of the barren winter, where nature is frozen
dead, and the storm rides on the gale, and the
earth is bare and naked, and the air is cold and
dreary, and the sun shines gloomily through the
bleak and murky skies, that sudden change could
not have been more keenly nor more painfully
felt than that which marked the contrast between
the southern lands of Spain and the countries of
France and Germany and England and Italy,
during the same age of the world's history.
Scarcely a city anywhere, save those few that
had been erected along the Rhine and the Danube by the Romans. Nothing that could, even
with the broadest stretch of leniency, be designated as agricultural. Everywhere pathless forests, howling wastes, ill-boding wildernesses,
death-exhaling swamps, pestiferous fens. Prus-
sia, and many more of to-day's proudest stars
in the galaxy of European provinces, we find still
uncivilized, still roaming about in the very cos-
tumes of native barbarians, in the spirits—and vam-
pires—and nixes—and gnomes—and kobolds—
inhabited pathless forests. Nowhere a street or
highway, save those the Romans had built.
Everywhere we must make our way, amidst indescribable difficulties, through almost impassable
mud and clay. The people crowded together in
miserable hamlets, inhabit wretched homesteads,

crudely and bunglingly put together of undressed timber, or of twigs wattled together and covered with clays or thatched with straw or reeds, consisting seldom of more than one room, which shelters alike man, woman, child, man servant, maid servant, fowl and beast, a commingling of sex and species not altogether conducive to modesty or morality. The floor, for the main part is composed of the hard bare ground, or at best is covered with dry leaves or with filthy rushes. Nowhere a window, nowhere a chimney, the smoke of the ill-fed, cheerless fire escaping through a hole in the roof. Straw pellets constitute the bed, and a round log serves the place of bolster and pillow, one platter of treen stands in the center of the table—if "table" it might be called— from which man, woman and child, master and servant, maid and mistress, eat with spoons of wood. Fingers serve the place of knives and forks, and a wooden trencher makes the round to quench the thirst.

Everywhere we meet with men with squalid beards, and women with hair unkempt and matted with filth, and both, clothed in garments of untanned skin, or, at best, of leather or hair cloth, that are not changed till they drop in pieces of themselves, a loathsome mass of vermin, stench and rags. No attempt at drainage; the putrefying slops and garbage and rubbish are unceremoniously thrown out of the door.

The most revolting uncleanness abounds, and we cannot help thinking of the scrupulous cleanliness that distinguished Cordova, for cleanness is

one of the most rigorous injunctions and requirements with both the religion of Mohammed and
the religion of Moses.   Here, on the contrary,
personal uncleanliness, the renunciation of every
personal comfort, the branding of every effort for
better surroundings, we are told, upon inquiry,
has the highest sanction of the church.   The sordid example set by the Ascetic monks has established the belief that cleanliness of the body leads
to the pollution of the soul, that in the past those
saints were most admired who had become one
hideous mass of clotted filth.   With a thrill of
admiration a priest informs us that St. Jerome had
seen a monk who for thirty years had lived in a
hole, and who never washed his clothes, nor
changed his tunic till it fell to pieces; that St.
Ammon had never seen himself naked; that the
famous virgin, named Silvia, had resolutely refused
for sixty years, on religious principles, to wash
any part of her body, except her fingers; that
St. Euphraxia had joined a convent of 130 nuns,
who shuddered at the mention of a bath; that an
anchorite had once imagined that he was mocked
by an illusion of the devil, as he saw gliding before him through the desert a naked creature
black with filth and years of exposure; it was the
once beautiful St. Mary of Egypt, who had thus
during forty-seven years been expiating her sins
of Asceticism."

We have seen enough to lead us to the conclusion, that when we enter into an examination
of the mental and moral and religious state of
the people, whose personal and domestic life

hold so low a rank in the history of civilization, we must not place our expectations too high. But low as we picture it to ourselves, the reality we find is infinitly lower than even our most lenient imagination had pictured it. Only a week ago we found Cordova proud, and distinguished, and peerless in the realm of culture, and art, and philosophy, and science, and now, during the same period of the world's history, we find a deep black cloud of appalling ignorance overhanging France, and Italy, and Germany and England, here and there only broken by a few, a very few, glimmering lights. Intellect, fettered hand and foot, lies bleeding at the feet of benighted barbarism, writhing in pain beneath the lashes of degrading superstitions, and groveling credulity. We search for the cause of this stupendous ignorance, and we soon find that to the clergy, more than to all other causes combined, belongs the very ignoble distinction of having ushered into Europe this stolid ignorance, and for being responsible for the unatonable crime of having retarded the advance of civilzation by many centuries.

To the all powerful and all controlling influence of the Church is to be ascribed the universal paralysis of the mind during the very same period, when art and science and independent research flourished in Southern Spain under Moorish and Jewish influence. Whomsoever we approach, be they dignitaries of the Church or Church menials, distinguished luminaries or obscure parish priests, a conversation

with them soon proves to us the sad truth, that
their stock of knowledge exhausts itself with an
enumeration of some monstrous legends or
with the practice and teaching of some degrading
and repulsive superstitions.

Secular knowledge is spurned.   Physical
science is held in avowed contempt and persecuted upon the ground of its inconsistency with
revealed truth.   Philosophical research is prohibited, under the severest punishment, as perni-
cions to piety.   Upon inquiry as to the cause of
this persecution of learing on the part of the church,
which, as we modestly dare to suggest, has nothing to lose, but everything to gain from rational
research and diligent pursuit of knowledge, a
bishop emphatically informs us that they did this
with the sanction and authority of the fourth
council of Carthage, which had prohibited the
reading of secular books by bishops, and with the
authority of Jerome who had condemned the
study of secular subjects, except for pious ends,
and as there was no lack of piety (so they artless-
ly thought) they saw little use in preserving the
learning and literature of the accursed Jews and
heathens, and fearing lest they fall into the hands
of others, not so pious as they, and not so pro-
tected against their pernicious influence by the
knowledge of legends, or by the skillful use of
magic spells, or exorcising charms, as they were.
Or perhaps secretly fearing, lest an intimate
knowledge of the learning of the ancients might
open the eyes of the people to the ignorance and
extortions and crimes and corruptions of the

Church, they condemn that whole literature to the flames. Hundreds and thousands of valuable manuscripts are thus pitilessly destroyed. We fain would stay their cruel hand, but we fear for our lives. We see them erase the writing from hundreds and thousands of parchment copies of ancient priceless lore, and substitute in its stead legends of saints, and ecclesiastical rubbish, occasioning thus the loss of many an ancient author that is now so painfully missed.

We turn away from this revolting stupidity, but nowhere a pleasing sign to allay our anguish, or appease our grief-stricken heart.

"Oh, thou monstrous ignorance, how deformed dost thou look."

Nowhere freedom of humane thought. Everyone compelled to think as ecclesiastical authority orders him to think. In Germany, France and Northern Spain we find scarcely one priest out of a thousand who can write his name. In Rome itself, once the city of art and culture and learning, as late as 992, a reliable authority informs us, there is not a priest to be found who knows the first elements of letters. In England, King Alfred informs us that he cannot recollect a single priest south of the Thames (then the most civilized part of England) who at the time of his accession understood or could translate the ordinary Latin prayer, and that the homilies which they preached were compiled for their use by some bishop from former works of the same kind, or from the early Patristic writings. Throughout Christendom we

find no restraint on the ordination of persons absolutely illiterate, no rules to exclude the ignorant
from ecclesiastical preferment, no inclination and
no power to make it obligatory upon even the
mitred dignitaries, to be able to read a line from
those Scriptures which they are to teach and
preach as the rule of right and the guide to moral
conduct.   Darkness, intense darkness, stupendous ignorance everywhere.   We shudder as we
think of the cruelties which this ignorance will be-
queath as its curse upon mankind.   We shudder
as we think of how this ignorance needs must
check the advance of civilzation.   We know
that knowledge will not be fettered forever, but
before it shall be able to assert its right to sway
over the mind of men, countless giant minds will
have to be crushed and indescribable suffering will have to be endured.   We know
that "ignorance seldom vaults into knowledge,
but passes into it through an intermediate state
of obscurity, even as night into day through twilight."   We tremble for those independent spirits
that shall live during that transitory period.   That
twilight will be reddened by the reflection of
streams of human blood.

We fain would speed away from these European
lands, for we instinctively feel that we are in lands
under the curse of God, and smitten with darkness,
because their people had laid cruel hands upon
the lands and the people of learning and culture
and art.

But we must stay.   We must note, distressing
though the duty be, the terrible influence which

this ignorance exercised upon the morals of the Church itself, and upon the mental and moral and political and social and industrial state of the people.

CHAPTER III.

EUROPE DURING THE DARK AGES.
(CONTINUED.)

GROSS SUPERSTITIONS.—A CRUCIFIX THAT SHED TEARS OF BLOOD.—THE
VIRGIN'S HOUSE CARRIED THROUGH THE AIR BY ANGELS.—SATAN
IN THE FORM OF A BEAUTIFUL WOMAN.—SCENES IN HELL.
THE BURNING OF WITCHES.—A KING WHO CANNOT WRITE
HIS NAME.—FEUDAL LORDS AS HIGHWAY ROBBERS
THE SERFDOM OF THE PEASANTS
RETURN TO CORDOVA

We promised to make a careful examination into the influence which the ignorance of the clergy exercised upon the aspect of religion, upon the morals of the Church, and upon the social, industrial, political, moral and mental state of the people at large. We fear we made a rash promise. So heartrending are the sights we see, if we are to give a faithful report, those unacquainted with the state of European civilization during the period which we are traversing, we fear, may accuse us of exaggeration, or worse still, may think that we, who belong to the race that suffered most during that period from the corruption of the Church, are animated by a spirit of revenge, and, therefore, find intense delight in holding so revolting a picture before our readers. But, happily, our readers are not composed of such. We are addressing intelligent people, men and women who know that our people have suffered too terribly and too unjustly from false accusations during many, many centuries, to render ourselves guilty of the same crime; men and women who know, that it is not from choice, but from historic necessity, that we contrast the social, and moral and intellectual state of Christian Europe during the Dark Ages, with the social and moral and intellectual state of Moorish and Jewish Europe of the same period, to appreciate the better the wonderful civilization of "*The Jews and Moors in Spain.*"

Our search discloses to us the sad and terrible truth that ignorance, especially active ignorance, is the mother of superstition, and both the parents of fanaticism, and the offspring of this trio is deliberate imposture, extortion, corruption, crime, and these, in their turn, beget the world's misfortunes. This sad truth stares us in the face whatever church, cathedral, monastery or community we enter. Everywhere miracles and relics and idolatry. Everywhere the teaching and preaching of hell and Satan and witchcraft, and of the necessity of blind credulity and unquestioning belief. Every cathedral and monastery has its tutelar saint, and every saint his legend, and wondrous accounts are spread concerning the saint's power, for good or evil, often fabricated to enrich the church or monastery under his protection.

In Dublin we see the crucifix that sheds tears of blood. In Loretto we see the house once inhabited by the Virgin, and we were told, that some angels, chancing to be at Nazareth when the Saracen conquerors approached, fearing that the sacred relic might fall into their possession, took the house bodily in their hands, and, carrying it through the air, deposited it at its present place. In Bavaria they show us the brazen android which Albertus Magnus had so cunningly contrived as to serve him for a domestic, and whose garrulity had so much annoyed the studious Thomas Aquinas. In Alsace the abbot Martin shows us the following inestimable relics, which he had obtained for his monastery: a spot of the blood of Jesus, a piece of the true cross, the arm of the apostle James, part of the skeleton of John the Baptist, a bottle of milk of the blessed Virgin, and, with an ill-disguised envy, he told us that a finger of the Holy Ghost is preserved in a monastery at Jerusalem.

Everywhere we are told that the arch fiend and his innumerable legions of demons are forever hovering about us, seeking our present unhappiness and the future ruin of mankind; that we are at no time, and at no place, safe from them; that we cannot be sufficiently on our guard against them, for sometimes they assume the shape of a grotesque and hideous animal; sometimes they appear in the shape of our nearest and dearest relatives and friends: sometimes as a beautiful woman, alluring by more than human charms, the unwary to their destruction, and laying plots, which were but too often successful against the virtue of the saints; sometimes the Evil One assumes the shape of a priest, and, in order to bring discredit upon that priest's character, maliciously visits, in this saintly disguise, some very questionable places and allows himself to be caught in most disgraceful situations and environments. Can we imagine an invention more ingenius to hide the foul practices of the corrupt among the clergy?

Everywhere the clergy finds it a very profitable traffic to teach how the people might protect themselves against the Evil One. The sign of the cross, a few drops of Holy water, the name of the Virgin, the Gospel of St. John around the neck, a rosary, a relic of Christ or of a saint, suffice to baffle the utmost efforts of diabolic malice, and to put the Spirits of Evil to an immediate and ignominious flight.

There is not a Church, not a monastery that we enter, but that our blood is chilled at its fountain, as we gaze upon the ghastly paintings, representing the horrible tortures of hell, placed conspicuously for the contemplation of the faithful, or for the fear of the wicked, or for the gain of the clergy—for the heavier the purse the church receives, the surer the release. It is impossible to conceive more ghastly conceptions of the future world than these pictures evinced, or more hideous calumnies against that Being, who was supposed to inflict upon His creatures such unspeakable misery. On one picture the devil is represented bound by red-hot chains, on a

burning gridiron in the center of hell.   His hands
are free, and with these he seizes the lost souls,
crushes them like grapes against his teeth, and
then draws them by his breath down the fiery
cavern of his throat.   Demons with hooks of red-
hot iron, plunge souls alternately into fire and ice.
Some of the lost are hung by their tongues,
others are sawn asunder, others are gnawed by
serpents, others are beaten together on an anvil,
and welded into a single mass, others are boiled
and strained through a cloth, others are twined
in the embraces of demons whose limbs are of
flames.   But not only the guilty are represented
suffering thus, but also the innocent, who expiate
amidst heartrending tortures the guilt of their
fathers.*   A little boy is represented in his suffering.   His eyes are burning like two
burning coals.   Two long flashes come out
of his ears.   Blazing fire rolls out of his
mouth.   An infant is represented roasting in a
hot oven.   It turns and twists, it beats its head
against the roof of the oven in agony of its suffering.

Unable to gaze upon the scene of innocent suffering any longer, we turn from it, trembling
with rage.   We ask a priest, who chances to be
near, what fiend could calumniate thus the good
God?   And smoothly he replies:

"God was very good to this child.   Very likely God saw it would get worse and worse and
would never repent, and so it would have to be
punished much more in hell.   So God, in his

---

*Consult Wall's History of Infant Baptism.

mercy, called it out of the world in its early child-hood." †

We no longer wonder at the stupidity of the people, at the enormous wealth, and still greater power of the clergy, when we remember that the people were inoculated with the belief that the clergy alone could save them from such etern-al tortures, and that money was the safest and most potent redeemer, and the never failing media-tor for effacing the most monstrous crimes, and for securing ultimate happiness.

We turn from these frightful sights only to en-counter more terrible scenes of misery. So far we had gazed upon purely. imaginary suffering, now we encounter the real, the intensely real. Every-where we see the sky lurid from the reflection of the *autos da fe*, on which thousands of innocent-ly accused victims, suffer the most agonizing and protracted torments, without exciting the faintest compassion. Everywhere we hear the prison walls re-echo the piercing shrieks of women, suffering the tortures preceding their conviction as witches. And once, it was in Scotland, we were the unfortunate spectators of a sight which we never shall forget. While the act of burning witches was being preformed amidst religious ceremonies, with a piercing yell some of the wo-men, half burnt, broke from the slow fire that consumed them, struggled for a few moments with despairing energy among the spectators,

† For full account of the teaching of the Church during the Dark Ages concerning the suffering in hell, see Lecky's "History of European Morals," chap iv.

until, with wild protestations of innocence, they sank writhing in agony, breathing their last.

And why are these women burnt by the thousands, everywhere, in Germany, France, Spain, Italy, Flanders, Sweden, England, Scotland and Ireland? Because they had entered into a deliberate compact with Satan. They had been seen riding at midnight through the air on a broomstick or on a goat. They had worked miracles—thus infringing upon the monopoly of the saints—or had afflicted the country with comets, hailstorms, plagues, or their neighbors with disease or barrenness. And who invents so malicious a falsehood? Often the victims themselves, for, suspected or accused of witchcraft they are at once subjected to tortures, to force a confession of their guilt, and these are so terrible, that death is a release, and so they confess, whatever the witch-courts want them to confess. Many a husband cuts thus the marriage tie which his church had pronounced indissoluble. Many a dexterous criminal directs a charge of witchcraft against his accuser, and thus escapes with impunity.

Everywhere we find the whole body of the clergy, from pope to priest, busy in the chase for gain; what escapes the bishop is snapped up by the archdeacon, what escapes the archdeacon is nosed and hunted down by the dean, while a host of minor officials prowl hungrily around these great marauders. To give money to the priest is everywhere regarded as the first article of the moral code. In seasons of sickness, of danger, of sorrow, or of remorse, whenever the fear or the conscience of the worshiper is awakened he is. taught to purchase the favor of the saint. St. Eligus gives us this definition of a good Christian: "He who comes frequently to church, who presents an oblation that it may be offered to God on the altar, who does not taste the fruits of his land till he has consecrated a part of them to God, who offers presents and tithes to churches, that on the judgment day he may be able to say: "Give unto us Lord for we have given unto Thee;" who redeems his soul from punishment, and finally who can repeat the creeds or the Lord's prayer."

Bad as we find their greed, we find their moral corruption indescribably worse   Void of every sting of conscience, drunken, lost in sensuality and open immorality.   In Italy, a bishop informs us, that were he to enforce the canons against unchaste people administering ecclesiastical rites, no one would be left in the Church, except the boys.   Everywhere, clergymen, sworn to celibacy, take out their *"culagium,"* their license to keep concubines, and more than one council, and more than one ecclesiastical writer we find speaking of priestly corruption far greater than simple concubinage, prominently among whom they mention, Pope, John XXIII. abbot elect of St. Augustine, at Canterbury, the abbot of St. Pelayo, in Spain, Henry III Bishop of Liege, and they enumerate the countless nunneries, that are degraded into brothels, and are flagrant for their frequent infanticides.

There is scarcely a need for our reporting

concerning the influence, which this moral de-
pravity of the Church has upon the masses. We
find that the ignorance and the corruption and
the bigotry made the people fully as ignorant and
corrupt and vicious.   The pernicious doctrine already adopted in the fourth century, that it is an
act of virtue to deceive and lie, when by that
means the interests of the church might be pro
moted," ‡ leads the people to the conclusion
that nothing can be possibly wrong, which leads
to   the   promotion of the Church's interests
and   finances.   And so crimes are perpetrated, wrongs committed, deceptions practiced.
vice indulged without a pang of conscience, or a
throb of the gentler emotions.   Ignorance dead-
ens every finer feeling, and religion, instead of
elevating man's moral nature, crushes it by the
opportunities it offers for canceling crime with
money, and for saving the soul from eternal torture
and damnation by increasing the clergy's opportunities for debauchery.

We next look for the intellectual accomplishments, but we look in vain.   The masses are intensely ignorant.   The clergy can not instruct
them, neither would they, if they could.   Knowledge among the masses would have seriously
interfered with their all-controlling power, as it
really did in later centuries.   This ignorance is
fully shared by the secular chiefs of the land.
Kings repudiate book-learning as unworthy of
the crown, and warlike nobles despise it as disgraceful to the sword.   It is a rare thing, and

‡ "Mosheim's Ecclesiastical History "

not considered an accomplishment, to find a warrior who can read or write.   To suppose that he
can write is to insult him by mistaking him for
an ecclesiastic.   No less a personage than Phil-
ippe le Bel, the powerful monarch of United
France who conducts foreign wars and exter-
minates the Templars, signs his name with the
sign of the cross or a rude arrow head, as late as
the thirteenth century.   Let us not forget, that
nearly three hundred years earlier in the world's
history, we had found public schools, academies,
universities, libraries, poets, artists, scientists and
philosophers flourishing among the Moors and
Jews of Cordova—had   seen Al Hakem the
Caliph, writing a digest on the fly-leaves of the
contents of each of his books in his great library.
We next look for the Industries, and there is
little to be found that can be honored with that
name.   A belief prevails among the people that
the millenium, the end of the world, will set in,
amidst terrible sufferings at the year 1000.   This
belief stifles industry, and property and wealth
are turned over to the Church for the sake of the
soul's release   Next   come   the Crusades and
these sap Europe of the flower of its people,
who leave by the thousands and hundreds of
thousands (and of which numbers but few return), to keep the Moslems out of Jerusalem, while
the aged and the infirm, the women and children,
eke out a miserable existence at home, feeding
on beans, vetches, roots, bark of trees—often
horseflesh and mare's milk furnish a delicious

repast. During the intervals between the various Crusades those few who return, are so accustomed to their roving and plundering life that it is impossible for them to settle down to mechanical or industrial pursuits.

The Jews devote themselves almost exclusively to the industries, and for this they suffer much. Commerce is not safe. The feudal lords descend from their fortresses to pillage the merchant's goods. The highways are besieged by licensed robbers, who confiscate the merchandise, murder the owners, or sell them as slaves, or exact enormous ransoms. Might makes right, and the most-powerful are the most distinguished for their unscrupulous robberies. Their castles, erected on almost inaccessible heights among the pathless woods, become the secure receptacles of predatory bands, who spread terror over the country and make traffic and enterprise insecure and next to impossible. And as it is on land so it is at sea, where a vessel is never secure from an attack of the pirates, and where neither restitution nor punishment of the crimnals is obtained from governments, which sometimes fear the plunderer and sometimes connive at the offense.

The political state of Europe we find still worse. The word *liberty* has not yet found its way into the dictonaries of the people. By far the greater part of society is everywhere bereaved of its personal liberty.

Everyone that is not Noble is a slave. Warfare is the rule of the day. The Church tramples upon

kings and nobles ; these, in their turn, such is
the prestige of the feudal system, tyrannize over
the next lower order, the next lower order apes
the example of its superior upon its inferior, and
so on from lower to lower caste, till the lowest,
the peasants, who have sunk into a qualified
slavery called serfdom.   The fight for supremacy
between Church and State, the dreadful oppres-
sion of the several orders of feudalism, convulses
society with their perennial feuds, the pride of
the countries are either cruelly butchered or employed more frequently in laying waste the fields
of their rivals, or putting the destructive fire-
brand, or the ruthless sword upon the prosperity
of their foe, than improving their own.

Let this report, meager as it is, suffice.   The
ignorance and misery and suffering and cruelties
that abound everywhere are too revolting to
tempt a longer stay.   Like Ajax, we pray for
light.   Away from the jaws of darkness.

Ye sailors, ho! furl your sails, raise the anchor,
clear the harbor.   And thou goodly vessel,
staunch and strong, hie thee straight across the
foaming deep.   And thou, O Aeolus, blow cheer-
ily and lustily thy sonthern winds upon us.   And
thou, O Neptune, speed thou our course, haste
us back again to fair Andalusia, to beauteous
Cordova, for there is no spot on earth like Cordova, "the city of the seven gates," "the tent of
Islam," "the abode of the learned," "the meeting
place of the eminent" the city of parks and palaces, aqueducts and public baths, the city of
chivalrous knights and enchanting ladies.

Aeolus and Neptune answer our prayer. The goodly ship she spins along. "She walks the waters like a thing of life."   Soon the lands we eager seek will be descried, and, once again upon the sunny shore, we shall continue our observations, and freely share them with our friend upon Columbia's virgin soil.

CHAPTER IV.

OUR RETURN TO CORDOVA.

CORDOVA AT DAY-BREAK.—THE MOHAMMEDAN SABBATH.—THE YOUTH
OF CORDOVA DISPORTS ITSELF UPON THE WATER.—SONG.—CHAL-
LENGE BETWEEN OARSMAN.—THE MUEZZIN'S CALL.—THE
GREAT MOSQUE.—A SERMON.—CHASDAI IBN SHAPRUT,
THE JEWISH MINISTER TO THE CALIPH. —DUNASH
IBN LABRAT.—ON THE WAY TO ABDALLAH
IBN XAMRI, THE MOORISH POET.

Again our light-winged boat glides upon the
broad and silvery bosom of the majestic Guadal-
quiver, along parks filled with flowering shrubs,
along glittering palaces and song-resounding
woods, along palmy islets, and sweet scented and
crimson-tinted hills.

It is an early spring morning, nearly 1,000
years back in the world's history. Our boat
makes a sudden turn, and Cordova, all glisten-
ing in the morning dew, raises her head as if
from a bath in the crystal stream. Aurora, god-
dess of the dawn, blushes in the sky, and with
her rosy fingers she sports playfully with the
golden tresses of Andalusia's fairest daughter.
It is morn,

"When the magic of daylight awakes
A new wonder each moment, as slowly it breaks;
Hills, cupolas, fountains, called forth everyone
Out of darkness, as if but just born of the sun."

It is with difficulty that our agile oarsman, the raven-locked and graceful featured jewish youth, whose services as guide we have again secured, makes his way among the countless pleasure boats that ply to and fro. We marvel at this, for distinctly we remember how the broad stream was furrowed during our first visit by boats of traffic only. "It is Friday, the Mohammedan Sabbath," our guide informs us, and we no longer wonder. The boats, some gilded, some festooned, some decked with the richest tapestry, are peopled with gay and happy pleasure seekers. The whole youth of Cordova seems to disport itself upon the water. The air re-echoes their merry laughters and their music:

"From psaltery, pipe and lutes of heavenly thrill
Or there own youthful voices, heavenlier still."

The winged chorister of the woods and parks take up the refrain, and warble their sweetest, as if in contest with voices human for supremacy in song. But what is most strange and most charming is the continual challenge between the oarsmen for repartee songs, which are either extemporized at the moment, or quotations from their numerous poets. A boat crosses our path, stays our course, and its oarsman to test our guide's readiness to sing Cordova's praise, thus begins in the sweet tones of the poetic Arabic tongue:

"Do not talk of the court of Bagdad and its glittering magnificence
Do not praise Persia and China, and their manifold advantages.
For there is no spot on earth like Cordova,
Nor m the whole world beauties likes its beauties."

To which our guide instantly replies, with a sweet and pure tenor voice:

> "O, my beloved Cordova!
> Where shall I behold thine equal.
> Thou art like an enchanted spot,
> Thy fields are luxuriant gardens,
> Thy earth of various colors
> Resembles a flock of rose colored amber."

The challenging oarsman had meet his peer. He is pleased with the reply and clears the path. Now our oarsman impedes the path of a boat, and taking for his theme, "The Ladies," challenges its oarsman thus:

> "Bright is the gold and fair the pearl,
> But brighter, fairer, thou, sweet girl.
> Jacinths and emeralds of the mine,
> Radiant as sun and moon may shine,
> But what are all their charms to thine?" ·

To which the challenged replies:

> "The Maker's stores have beauties rare,
> But none that can with thee compare,
> O pearl, that God's own hand hath made;
> Earth, sky and sea,
> Compare with thee,
> See all their splendors sink in shade."

We have reached the landing place. Again we tread in the streets of Cordova, that had surprised and delighted us so much during our first visit. We have not advanced far, when suddenly there breaks on our ear a voice, loud and mighty, as never heard before. We look in the direction whence the voice comes, and on the graceful balcony around the "minaret"—the "muezzin," who calleth, with a solemn power in his living voice, which neither flag, trumpet, bell nor fire could simulate or rival, the Faithful thus to prayer:

"Come to prayer! Come to prayer! Come to the Temple of Salvation! Great God! Great God! There is no God except God!"

At the sound of the *muezzin's* call, the throngs that crowd the streets hasten their steps, while some few stop, and turning towards the Kiblah— (point of the heaven in the direction of Mecca, which is indicated by the position of the minarets,) either prostrate themselves upon the ground, or, folding their arms across their bosom, bow their turbaned head to the ground, and raise their heart and voice to Allah. Five times, every day, our guide informs us, the *muezzin* calls the faithful to prayer. Those who are thus worshiping publicly upon the streets, are for some reasons prevented from attending the mosque, and the Koran allows them to pray in any clean place, and the streets of Cordova are clean indeed. Prayer is great with the Moors, our guide continnes. Mohammed has laid great stress upon its efficacy and importance. "It is the pillar of religion and the key to paradise," said he "Angels come among you both by night and day, when they ascend to heaven God asks them how they left his creatures. We found them, say they, at their prayers, and we left them at their prayers." Even the postures to be observed in prayer he had prescribed. Females in prayer are not to stretch forth their arms, but to hold

them on their bosoms.   They are not to make as
deep inflexions as the men.   They are to pray
in a low and gentle tone of voice.   They are not
permitted to accompany the men to the mosque,
lest the mind of the worshipers should be drawn
from their devotions.   Neither are they allowed
to worship together with the men.   They have
their gallery in the mosque fenced in with latticework.   No one is permitted to go to prayer
decked with costly ornaments or clothed in sump-
tuous apparel.

While listening to our guide, our feet unconsciously followed the hastening throngs,
and before we were aware of it we stood before
the "mezquita," the great mosque, the famous
edifice which, with its buildings and courts, covers more space than any place of worship in
existence, the rival of the *Caaba* at Mecca, and
of the *Alaska* of jerusalem.   Like all Moorish
architecture, its exterior is very plain.   Our guide
gives us its dimensions; it is 642 feet long and 440
wide.   The height of the Alminar tower is 250 feet.

This is Friday, the "*Yawn al Yoma*," the great
day of assembly for worship, the Mohammedan
Sabbath, sacred because on that day man was
created, because that day had already been consecrated by the early Arabains to "Astarte," Venus,
the most beautiful of the planets and the brightest of the stars; and, also because from that day,
Friday (july 16, 622,) the day of the *Hegira*, begins the Mohammedan calender.   Our guide assures us that there are special service on Friday)
that on this day the *Mufti* expounds some chap-

ters from the Koran, and the *"Imaum"* (preacher,) delivers a *Khotbeh"* (sermon).

We enter through one of the nineteen lofty and massive bronze gates, and the beauties we now behold baffle description.

The *"Kiblah"* is reached by nineteen aisles, marked by columns of jasper, beryl, verd-antique, porphyry, finely carved, supporting in two directions double horse-shoe arches, one above the other. These are crossed by thirty-eight aisles, also composed of columns of different marbles, making thus literally a forest of columns. The ceiling is filled with ovals inscribed with appropriate inscriptions from the Koran, to call the mind of the faithful to contemplation and devotion. From it are suspended 280 chandeliers, which light the vast space with upwards of 10,000 lights.

The *"Al Mihrab,"* at the *"Kiblah"* end of the mosque is an octagonal niche, the ceiling of which is formed like a shell out of a single block of white marble. Within it is the Shrine of Shrines, containing one of the original copies of the Koran, the one which lay upon the lap of *Othman,* the third Caliph, our guide tells us, when he was assassinated; it is stained with his life blood. It lies upon a lecturn of aloe wood, put together with golden nails. The doors of the shrine are pure gold, the floor solid silver, inlaid with gold and *lapis lazuli.* In front of it is the pulpit made of costly woods, inlaid with ivory and enriched with jewels; the nails joining its parts are also of gold and silver. It is the gilt of

the Caliph, and the cost exceeds $1,000,000.
The Caliph himself drew t1e plan of the entire
edifice, and assisted daily with his own hands in
its erection.

Within the mosque there is a court 220 feet
long, containing promenades which invite to de-
vout meditations, and reservoirs and fountains
for their ablution, for, as our guide informs us, ablution is enjoined by the Koran, with great precission
as preparative to prayer; purity of body being
considered emblematical of purity of soul.

T1ere is not a seat in the entire edifice; the
worshipers are either prostrated upon the floor,
whic1 is artistically paved with marble mosaics,
or they stand profoundly bent in reverence.*

As t1e Mufti, his careful ablutions being completed, approaches the *"Al Mihrab,"* to take
from its sacred Shrine the copy of the Koran, all
prostrate themselves on the ground.   He opens
the book, and with a loud voice he reads the first
"sura," chapter:

"Bismillah"—in the name of the most merciful God.   Praise be to God, the Lord of all creatures, the Most Merciful, the King of the Day of
judgment.   Thee do we worship, and of Thee do
we beg assistance.   Direct us in the right way,
in the way of those to whom Thou hast been gra-
cions; not of those against whom thou art in-
censed, not of those who go astray."

* For detailed description of the "Great Mezquita," see Conde's
"History of the Arabs in Spain," Vol. I, Chapter XXXIV, and Coppee's
"Conquest in Spain," Book X, Chapter V; for Belief and Woiship," see
Conde, and Irving's "Mahomet," appendix to volume I.

To which the whole congregation responds:

"God, there is no God but He, the Living, the Ever Living; He sleepeth not, neither doth He slumber. To Him belongeth the Heavens and the earth, and all that they contain. He knoweth the Past and the Future, but no one can comprehend anything of this knowledge but that which He revealeth. His sway extendeth over the Heavens and the Earth, and to sustain them both is no burden to Him. He is the high, the mighty. There is no God besides Him, and "*Mohammed Resul Allah*" Mohammed is the prophet of God."* The *Mufti* now expounds a chapter from the Koran, and at the end of each of its lessons the whole congregation responds, 'Amin!" "So be it."

The "*Imaum*" ascends the pulpit to preach his sermon. He bases his theme upon the chapter just expounded. He speaks of faith and practice, of faith in God, in his angels, in his Koran, in his prophets, in the resurrection and final judgement, in predestination. "Angels," he says," keep continual watch upon each mortal, one on the right hand, the other on the left, taking note of every word or action. At the close of each day they fly up to heaven to write up their report. Every good action is recorded ten times by the good angel on the right, and if the mortal commit a sin the same benevolent spirit says to the angel on the left: "Forbear for seven hours to record it; peradventure he may repent and pray and obtain forgiveness."

*Korau, part of Sura II.

He enjoins a reverence for the *Al Koran,* and
a scrupulous obedience to its precepts.   In it are
written all the decrees of God, and all events past,
present or to come.   It had existed from all etern-
ity and was treasured up in the seventh heaven,
and its contents were finally revealed to Mohammed by the Angel Gabriel.

He speaks of Adam, Noah, Abraham, Moses,
jesus, as prophets subordinate to Mohammed,
whose life and preceipts are worthy of following.

He speaks of predestination, and says that every
event is predetermined by God, that the destiny
of every individual and the hour of his death are
irrevocably fixed, and can neither be varied nor
evaded, by any effort of human sagacity or
foresight.

He reconciles fate and free-will by saying:
"The outline is given us we color the picture of
life as we will."

He speakes of Charity, and says that every
one must dispense, in one way or the other, a
tenth of his revenue in the relief of the indigent
or distressed.   He speaks of the great virtue of
fasting and says: "Prayer leads us half way to
God, fastening conveys us to His threshold and
alms-conducts us into His presence."   He enjoins
the doing of good and the shunning of evil, and
above all an observance of the golden rule.

"If these precepts ye obey," he concludes, "the
pleasures of Paradise will be your reward.   There
you will be clothed in raiments sparkling with
jewels.   You will wear crowns of gold enriched
with pearls and diamonds, and dwell in sumptu-

ous palaces or silken pavilions, reclining in voluptuous couches. Hundreds of attendants, bearing dishes and goblets of gold, will serve you with every variety of exquisite viands and beverage, whenever and in whatever quantity you shall want them. There the air, fragrant with the sweetest perfume, resounds with the melodious voices of the Daughters of Paradise. There, besides your wives you had on earth, who will rejoin you in all their pristine charms, black-eyed *Hooreeyahs* (Houris) having complexions like rubies and pearls, resplendent beings, free from every human defect or frailty, perpetually retaining their youth and beauty, will constantly attend you, and cheerfully obey your wishes.

But woe unto you if ye harken not to the words of *Allah* and Mohammed his prophet! When ye shall pass the bridge, *Al Sirat*, which is finer than a hair and sharper than a sword, it will break beneath the burden of your sins, and precipitate you into the shadow and smoke and fire of hell."

With a prayer for the welfare of the Caliph and the entire government, the "khotbeh" is ended and the congregation dismissed.

We know that the Moors and jews are Oriental people, and, therefore, not indigenous to the Occidental soil they now inhabit. Whence came they? Why came they? We are eager for a correct answer to these questions, and knowing none of Cordova's learned men, we think of our distinguished co-religionist, *Abu Jussuf*

Chasdai ben Isaac Ibn Shaprut, the jewish Physician, Philologist, Minister of Foreign Affairs, of Commerce and Finance to the learned *Abder Rahman*, and *Nasi*, or secular chief, of all European jews. We take the heart to visit him, and with the aid of our guide, we soon are admitted into the house. There we learn that *Chasdai Ibn Shaprut* had just been summoned to a secret consultation with the Caliph concerning an important embassy that had come from *Otto I*, Emperor of Germany. We are asked to await his return in his library. There, we are introduced to *Moses ben Chanoch*, the distinguished Talmudist, to his pupil, *Joseph ben Abitur*, the translator of the *Mishnah* into Arabic for the Caliph's library, to *Menachem ben Saruk*, the grammarian and compiler of the first Hebrew lexicon, and to *Dunash ben Labrat*, the distinguished poet, who were pursuing their respective studies in the magnificent library of Chasdai, the jewish favorite Minister to the Caliph.

We state our wish, and Dunash ben Labrat thus replies:

"We know not when our distinguished *Nasi* will return. If, indeed, it be agreeable to you, I will ask you to accompany me to my friend *Abdallah Ibn Xamri*, the famous Moorish poet and erudite historian, with whom I have arranged a game of chess for this afternoon's siesta. He will, I know, give you such information concerning the history of the Arab-Moors as you may desire When this shall have been done, we shall make our way back again, Chasdai will have returned, and he will gladly give you an account of the Entrance of the jews into Spain."

We cheerfully accept his kind proposal. We are on our way now, and in the following chapter we shall faithfully report all that we shall see and hear.

CHAPTER V.

THE ARAB-MOORS.

ABDALLAH TELLS THE EARLY HISTORY OF THE ARABS.—MIRACLES AT
THE BIRTH OF MOHAMMED.—THE ANGEL, GABRIEL, WRITES
THE KORAN UPON PALM LEAVES.—TEN DECISIVE YEARS
IN THE HISTORY OF RELIGION —BEAUTIFUL
ZELICA.—ARAB-MOORS CHECKED IN
THEIR CONQUEST—QUARREL
BETWEEN KING ROD-
ERICK AND
COUNT JULIEN, FATHER OF THE INSULTED FLORINDA.—JEWS ALLY
WITH THE WRONGED FATHER.—ANDALUSIA CONQUERED.

In a beautiful valley on the banks of the Gaud-
alquivir, about five miles from Cordova, within
sight of the Caliph's magnificent palace of *Medi-
na-al-Zohar* (town of the flower) stands the pict-
uresque residence of the Moorish poet, Abdallah
Ibn Xamri. Dunash ben Labrat, the distinguished jewish poet, our new found friend and guide,
has no need for a formal announcement. A
massive bronze gate opens into a beautifully
paved court yard, from the center of which issues
the never-failing fountain jet to a dazzling height,
diffusing refreshing coolness and making a pleasant patter of the falling drops into the basin. A
gallery encircles this court, supported by slender

columns of alabaster, from which spring numbers of graceful horseshoe arches. The interspaces above the arches are filled with arabesques, inter-wreathing striking texts from the Koran in brilliant red and blue and gold. Above these are the latticed windows which light the seraglio.

From this luxurious court we pass through a double archway into another, abounding with tropical plants. Here within the concealment of the densest shade trees, is a very long oblong marble basin, supplied with artificially cooled water. Here, in the early morning and in the evening twilight, the indolent, the warm, the weary bathe in luxurious languor. Here the women meet to disport themselves, while the entrances are guarded by eunuchs against intrusion. From this private court a postern leads into a beautiful garden with mazy walks and blooming *parterres*, replete with artificial grottoes and kiosks of stained glass, and terraces of polished marbles, and balustrades supported by guilded columns, and ponds filled with gold and silver fishes.

"Here we shall find Abdallah Ibn Xamri," says Dunash ben Labrat; "he delights to take his siesta within yonder pavilion, which is well pro vided with books and musical instruments. There his beautiful daughter *Zelica* tunes the lyre as he courts the muses, and her melodious voice has inspired his most wondrous lyric gems."

Abdallah recognizes Dunash's voice, and bids him enter. We obey the summons. Surprise is visible in Abdallah's countenance as he gazes up-

on our strange faces.   Before us stands a typical
Moor.   His person is well formed.   He has an
oval face, aquiline nose, long and arched eye-
brow, nearly meeting, large restless black eyes,
smooth skin, clear olive complexion, full dark
hair and beard, and an elastic springy step.   His
head is covered with a green woolen cap of
cylindrical form from which hangs a blue tassel.
Over a long straight robe of light cloth, he wears a
shorter tunic, elaborately embroidered.   Sandals
are tied to his feet with strings of twisted silver
and gold.

We exchange *Salams*.   Our friend introduces
us.   In measured rhyme he states that he had
brought us to Cordova's distinguished son of the
muses to learn from the most authentic source
the "History of the entrance of the Arab-Moors into Spain." Abdallah receives us cordially, asks us
to recline upon the *divan*—the cushioned seats running along the walls of the pavilion—he takes
his re-clining position opposite us, and after a
few in-troductory remarks he speaks as follows:

"The great peninsula, formed by the Red Sea,
by the Euphrates, by the Gulf of Persia
and by the Indian ocean, and known by the
name of Arabia, is the birthplace of our creed.
It was peopled soon after the deluge by the children of *Shem*, the son of Noah.   In course of
time the brave *Yarab* established the kingdom
of *Yemen*, whence the Arabs derive the names
of themselves and their country.   During a long
succession of ages, extending from the earliest
period of recorded history down to the seventh

century, Arabia remained unchanged and unaffected by the events which convulsed the rest of Asia and shook Europe and Africa to their very center The occupations of the people were trade and agriculture. The former had ports along the coasts, and carried on foreign trade by means of ships and caravans. The nomadic Arabs were the more numerous of the two. The necessity of being always on the alert to defend their flocks and herds made these familiar from their infancy, with the exercise of arms. No one could excel them in the use of the bow, the lance and the scimitar, and the adroit and graceful management of the horse. They were more at home on horseback than on foot. The horse was their friend and companion. They lived and talked with him and lavished upon him their dearest affection, and both were capable of sustaining great fatigue and hardship. The Arabs possessed in an eminent degree the intellectual attributes of the Shemitic race. Penetrating sagacity, subtle wit, a ready conception, a brilliant imagination, a proud and daring spirit were stamped upon their sallow visage, and flashed from their dark and kindling eye. Our language, naturally poetic, made them poets and the most eloquent of men. They were generous and hospitable. Their deadliest foe, having once broken bread with them, could repose securely beneath the inviolable sancity of their tent. Their religion originally consisted of a belief in the unity of God, in future life, in the necessity of prayer and virtue. This was the creed of Abraham and was

brought to them by Ishmael and Hagar. In the
course of time it became contaminated with
Sabean star worship and Magian idolatry.

When Palestine was ravaged by the Romans,
and the city of jerusalem taken and sacked,
many of the jews took refuge among them, and
gradually many of the tenets of the jewish faith
and practices of the jewish worship were again
insensibly adopted by them. The same refuge
Arabia offered later to many Christians who
were fleeing from the persecutions of Rome, and
these also engrafted gradually, some of their rites
and ceremonies and beliefs upon the people.
The result was a mixture of religious beliefs, the
highest religious principles alternating with the
most degrading idolatries. There was no accepted creed, no unified faith.

A great reformer was needed, and the great
Allah sent his prophet, *Mohammed*, to establish
the only true faith: *Islmism* His birth was accompanied by signs and portents, announcing a
child of wonder.† At the moment of his coming
into the world, a celestial light, illuminated the
surrounding country, and the new-born child,
raising his eyes to heaven, exclaimed "God is
great! There is no God but God, and I am his
Prophet." Heaven and earth were agitated at
his advent. Palaces, and temples and mountains
toppled to the earth. The fires, sacred to Zo-
roaster, which had burned, without interruption
for upwards of a thousand years, were suddenly

† Talmud Babli in *Sotah 13 a*, speaks of a similar supernatural light at
the birth of Moses.

extinguished, and all the idols in the world fell down. Though his true Messiahship was thus made evident at his birth, and in his youth, he still waited to the age of fully ripened manhood before he made the attempt of establishing the creed, which the angel Gabriel, had written down for him upon palm leaves. But when the time had come for raising his own nation from fetichism, from the adoration of a meteoric stone, and from the basest idol worship, he awakened his people out of their religious and political torpor, kindled the fire of enthusiasm among them, and they thirsted after opportunities for contest and conquests.

When death took the sword from his hand ten years later, the whole world trembled at the very mention of his name.

Here Abdallah pauses in his narative. He touches a silver bell, and soon a maiden appears. This is the first time that we are permitted to gaze upon a Moorish woman's face; those we met in the streets or parks, or saw behind the latticework of the woman's gallery in the mosque, were always clothed in the mantilla, which encircled their entire form, and their faces were always hidden under the face veil, or under the horsehair vizard, which left but the eyes visible. She wears her hair braided. A light cap or cornet, adorned with gems, forms the covering for her head. The side locks are entwined with coral beads, hung loosely to chinck with

every movement. ' Full white muslin trousers are
tied at the ankle with golden strings that end in
merry little silver bells.' 'A long full-white mantle of transparent muslin covers the tight-fitting
vest and jacket of silk, both of brilliant colors,
and. embroidered and decorated with woven
gold. Around her neck and arms and wrists she
wears chains, necklaces and bracelets, of gold,
and of coral and pearls and amber.

He whispers something in her ear, and immediately she disappears, light as an angel shape. A
deep silence ensues. At that moment we think
not of Mohammed, the founder of a new faith
and the conqueror of the world, but of Zelica,
Abdallah's daughter. that beauteous maiden,
whose complexion vies with the rubies and white
jasmine flowers she wears more radiant still when
her dazzling eyes drooped, and when the scarlet
hue of innocence mantled her face as her glance
met the eyes of men and strangers.

Abdallah had ordered refreshments. Servants
appear and spread an embroidered rug upon the
floor. Upon it they place a low tray, set with
silver and fine earthenware, and provided with
the choicest of fruits, confections and sherbets
flavored with violet. Low cushions are placed
around it, upon which we, following the example
of our host and guide, seat ourselves with our
legs crossed. Before eating, a servant pours
water on our hands from a basin and ewer. The
meal begins with "Bismilah'" for grace. A very
interesting conversation, displaying great learning and much reading, is carried on between the

two poets, as to whether Cordova or Bagdad leads the world in literature, art, science, and philosophy. Abdalah champions Cordova, Dunash favors Bagdad, his native home.

The delicious repast is ended. The floor is cleared, Abdallah resumes his narrative.

"The successors of Mohammed," says he, "followed in the footsteps of our prophet. They passed beyond the confines of Arabia, and persecuted their work of converting the world, giving to the conquered the choice between the Koran, or Tribute, or Death. In less than fifty years after the Prophet's death, Syria, Palestine, Egypt, Mesopotamia, Persia, Armenia, Asia Minor had accepted the religion of Mohammed. In jerusalem a mosque stood on the site where once the temple of Solomon stood. In Alexandria the Mohammedans wrought direful vengeance on Christians for the crimes which the arrogant and fanatical St. Cyril had committed there two centuries before, by extirpating Grecian learning and by inciting his monks to murder the wise *Hypatia*.

The extreme northern part of Africa brought their armies to a sudden halt. Here they encounter two strong foes. First, the people called *Berbers* "the Noble," a tall, noble looking race of men, active, high-spirited and indomitable. They had the same patriarchal habits, the same Shemitic features, were equally skilled in the use of arms and the breeding and handling of horses, and so the Arabs believed them to be of their own race. This Northern coast of Africa has been called by the Romans, from the dark complexion of its people: *Mauritania*, and its people were called *Mooriscos*, or *Moors*. When the superior force of the Arabians compelled the Moors to submit at last, the conquerors and the conquered coalesced so completely, that in less than a decade the one could not be distinguished from the other.

"The second foe, however, who inhabited the Northern extremity of *Almagreb*, where the continent of Africa protrudes boldly to meet the continent of Europe, was not so easily overcome. The rock-built city of *Ceuta* was garrisoned by Spanish soldiers, and its brave commander, Count *Julian*, defied the ·valiant Amir *Musa Ibn Nosseyr*, the Hero of Two Continents. It seemed as if *Islamism* had reached its limit, that it would never set its foot upon beautiful Andalusia, at which it had so often cast its wistful eye. But *Allah* favored the onward march of the religion of the Prophet! The wrong done by the wicked *Roderick*, King of Spain, to the young and beautiful *Florinda*, daughter of Count *Julian*, the brave commander of *Ceuta*, opened Europe to the Arab-Moors. *"By the living God,"* exclaimed the insulted father. *"I will be revenged."*

He soon found willing allies, consisting of the nobles, who could no longer endure the despotism of King Roderick, and of the jews, who had been expelled from Spain. Encouraged by these allies Count *Julian* entered into negotiations with Amir *Musa* for the delivery of Spain into his hands. Musa accepted cheerfully.

"Long had the crimes of Spain cried out to Heaven:
At length the measure of offence was full.
Count Julian called the invader.   .   .   .
          .   .   Mad to wreak
His vengeance for his deeply injured child
On Roderick's head, an evil hour for Spain,
For that unhappy daughter, and himself.
Desperate apostate, on the Moors he called,
And, like a cloud of locusts, whom the wind
Wafts from the plains of wasted Africa,
The Mussulman upon Iberia's shores
Descends.   A countless multitude they came:
Syrian, Moors, Saracen, Greek renegade,
Persian, and Copt, and Latin, in one band
Of Islam's faith conjoined, strong in the youth
And heat of zeal, a dreadful brotherhood."

The valiant *Tarik* crossed with a selected force, the strait between the Pillars of Hercules, which is now named after him *"Gibr-al-Tarik"* (Gibraltar), "the rock of Tarik." On the 24th of july, 711, the two armies met at the river of Guadalete, not far from Xeres, and after a three days' battle a small force of picked men, the indomitable horsemen of the desert, routed 80,000 Spaniards, amidst terrible carnage. Tarik pressed eagerly forward. *Cordova, Malaga, Toledo, Merida,* surrendered after little or no opposition. In six years later the Arab-Moors were complete masters of Spain, and have been so unto this day."

Abdallah has ended his narrative. Unconsciously, it seems, he takes the lute at his side, and running his fingers over the strings, he strikes a few chords and finally, as if desirious of supplementing his version of the entrance of Arab-

Moors into Europe, he makes the lute accompany his recital of some of the songs and verses he had composed in commemoration of the victory of the Arab-Moors over fair Andalusia, and which have since become as popular in Bagdad and Antioch as in Cordova or Granada. We wish, but our wish is in vain, that *Zelica* might return to her wonted task, that her young and melodious voice might blend with the melting strains of the Moorish bard.

The heroic theme inspires Abdallah more and more. He begins to improvise. He defends *Florinda*, whom the Spaniards execrate, and name "*La Cava*"—"the Wicked." He sings of Roderick's entering the cave over which was written: "*The king who opens this cave and discovers its wonders will learn both good and evil,*" and, how upon entering it he read this fatal inscription on the walls: "*Unhappy King, thou hast entered in an evil hour. By strange nations thou shalt be dispossessed, and thy people degraded.*" He sings of the combat between Tarik and Roderick. He sings of the captive queen *Egilona*. He sings of the jealousy between Mousa and Tarik, and of other themes, heroic and beautiful.

The *muezzin's* summons to evening prayer stops his muse, and makes our hasty departure necessary, for it is Friday evening, and the distance to the synagogue is long. We part hastily. Before leaving, however, Abdallah exacts a promise from Dunash that he will send for him whenever Chasdai ben Isaac, the distinguish ed jewish Minister to the Caliph, shall tell us the *History of the Entrance of the Jews into Spain.*

RODERICK'S LAMENT.

A SPANISH NATIONAL BALLAD.

Translated by J G Lockhart

The host of Don Rodrigo were scattered in dismay,
When lost was the eighth battle, nor heart nor hope had they;
He, when he saw the field was lost, and all his hope was flown,
He turned him from his flying host and took his way alone,

His horse was bleeding, blind, and lame, he could no farther go,
Dismounted, without path or aim, the king stepped to and fro.
It was a sight of pity to look on Roderick,
For sore athirst and hungry he staggered faint and sick.

All stained and strewed with dust and blood, like to some smoulder-
ing brand
Pluck'd from the flame, Rodrigo shew'd.   His sword was in his
hand;
But it was hacked into a saw of dark and purple tint;
His jewell'd mail had many a flaw, his helmet many a dint.

He climbed unto a hill-top, the highest he could see,
Thence all about of that wild route his last long look took he.
He saw his royal banners where they lay drenched and torn,
He heard the cry of victory, the Arabs' shout of scorn.

He look'd for the brave captains that had led the hosts of Spain,
But all were fled except the dead, and who could count the slain?
Where'er his eyes could wander, all bloody was the plain;
And while thus he said the tears he shed ran down his cheeks like
rain:

"Last night I was the King of Spain, to-day no king am I;
Last night fair castles held my train, to-night where shall I lie;   •
Last night a hundred pages did serve me on the knee,
To-night not one I call my own, not one pertains to me.

"O luckless, luckless was the hour, and cursed was the day
When I was born to have the power of this great seigniory;
Unhappy me that I should live to see the sun go down this night,
O Death, why now so slow art thou, why fearest thou to smite?"

CHAPTER VI.

A SABBATH EVE IN CORDOVA.

THE SYNAGOGUE OF CORDOVA.—THE DAUGHTERS OF ISRAEL PREPARING
FOR THE SABBATH.—THE THRONE OF THE "NASI."—RABBI MOSES
BEN CHANOCH.—THE ELOQUENCE OF SILENCE.—A TEARFUL
SCENE.—THREE RABBIS TAKEN CAPTIVE BY PIRATES.
EVIL DESIGNS AGAINST CHANOCH'S YOUNG
AND BEAUTIFUL WIFE.—SOLD AS
SLAVE TO CORDOVA.—HIS
MIRACULOUS RISE.

A paved walk, guarded on each side by majestic cypress trees, winding its course along ter-
raced gardens and near refreshing fountains,
leads up to the lofty eminence on which stands
the only synagogue of Cordova. Almost breath-
less we reach the height. We express our surprise that the Synagogue, visited twice daily, and
thrice on the Sabbath day, should have been lo-
cated so inconveniently, to which our distinguished friend Dunash ben Labrat replies: "Such is
the custom in Israel, both Solomon* and Ezra†
have established the custom of building the Synagogue on a lofty eminence. and the Talmud
teaches: "The city whose houses are higher
than its houses of worship will be destroyed."‡

* Proverbs, i:21.   † Ezra. ix:9.   ‡ Talmud Babli Sabbath, 11 a

Before entering, we pause awhile to cast our eyes about us. Were we standing on Mount Moriah, of deathless memory, with the gorgeous temple of Solomon before us, and with the sacred scenery of Jerusalem and her environments about us, even such scenes could not have awed us more than those which fascinate our heart and mind on the temple-mount of Cordova, the brightest gem in the proud diadem of fair Andalusia.

At the foot of the mount glides the silvery Guadalquivir. The blushing sun is sinking behind the azure hills, and houses and synagogues and foliage and fountain and river, all are crimson tinted, while the fleecy cloudlets, that float in his radiant tracks, are resplendent with colors of purple and violet and gold and red. The evening star sparkles in the rosy sky so benignly, as if it were the eye of God, pleased at seeing His "chosen people" hasten to prostrate themselves before His footstool. The golden glimmering vapors, that rise from beneath the illumined horizon into infinite space, seem to vault over the Synagogue, as if bestowing celestial Sabbath blessing over its worshipers. All nature around us inspires to worship. The nightingales have begun their evening hymns, and the air is loud with the soft melting notes of the skylarks, who sing their sweet "Good Night" to the sunken sun. Our soul, too, is filled with a yearning to commune with God, and so we turn toward the synagogue.

Like the mezquita (mosque) its exterior facade

is plain and unnoteworthy. We enter the high
and spacious vestibule, and our eye is dazzled
with all the magnificence, with the harmonious
blending of colors, with the costly, but chaste
ornamentations. The cupola above admits a
free circulation of air, bringing the sweet frag-
rance of the surrounding gardens. On the one
side is heard the refreshing sound of the flowing
waters within the reservoirs for ablution, and
on the other side the soft splash from the fountain jets in the garden.

Within the synagogue proper, clusters of delicate columns of various marbles and of costly
woods, support double galleries, one above the
other, with lattice work in front, that the black-
eyed and raven-locked and comely-featured Hebrew women may not draw the mind of the worshipers beneath from their devotions. The galleries are empty now. The Hebrew women do
not attend the service of the Sabbath Eve.
They are at home awaiting the return of their
husbands, fathers, brothers, All day long have
they been busy in the preparation for the Sabbath.
The house has been put in order. The choicest
that means would allow and the market afford
has been secured and prepared for the festive
Sabbath meal. Upon the table, decked with
snow white linens, and with the tempting dishes,
burn the lights in the heavy silver candlesticks,
and the traditional seven-armed Sabbath lamp,
suspended from the center of the ceiling, having
been lighted with Sabbath benedictions by the
queen of the house, sheds a hallowed light over

mother, wife and daughter, who are attired in
their neatest, and whose countenances are flush-
ed from the day's busy task, and whose eyes
beam, and whose hearts beat with joyous expectations.

But we have strayed from the description of
the galleries of the synagogue to the women in
their homes. What wonder the Spanish jews
had need of their latticed railings!

The interspaces between the graceful horseshoe
arches and the ovals in the ceiling are delicately
pencilled with brilliant colors, and the walls are
filled with arabesques interwreathing appropriate
Hebrew texts.

The wall to the east, the direction towards
jerusalem, holds the *Haichal*, the shrine, in
which is kept the *Thora*, the parchment scrolls of
the Pentateuch.

The shrine is canopied by a wondrously designed shell-shaped covering, inlaid with mother-
of-pearl, ivory and silver. A curtain of silk and
woven gold, and decorated with gems of chryso-
lite and emerals and sapphires, serves as a screen
to this "Holy of Holies." Over this shell-shaped
canopy is an illuminated window of artistic work
manship, inscribed in brilliant colors with the
words, "*Yehi Or,*" "Let there be light." The
moon, queen of the night, rides in the cloudless
sky, and she sends her peerless light through
this double-triangled window, and the effect is
most sublime.

Suspended from the ceiling, and directly in
front of the curtain is the *Ne'er Tamid* the "Per-

petual Lamp," famous for its wondrous beauty
and for its priceless value, the gift of the mother
of *Chasdai ben Isaac*, and its mellow light
sends a hallowing influence over the congregants.
Beneath it are the pyramidal steps, from which
the descendants of the High-Priest Aaron bestow,
on the great holidays, the priestly blessings upon
the congregation.   To the right and left of these
stand the *M'noroth*, the high seven-armed cande-
labra, a faithful copy of the Biblical design†.

In front of the steps stands the throne-like
chair, in which is seated *Chasdai ben Isaac*, the
Nasi, secular head of all European jews, the
Resh Kallah, President of the Academy for the
Talmudical Sciences at Pumbadita in Babylonia,
the Minister of Foreign Affairs, and of Commerce,
and of Finance to the Caliph Abderrahman III.

To the right of the shrine, on a raised platform, are seated Rabbi *Moses ben Chanoch*, the
Dayan, the chief judge and chief rabbi of all
European jews; at his right the *Sh'liach Hazibur*,
the Reader, is seated; at his left his Chief As-
sistant Dayan; at his feet sit the most advanced
disciples of his far-famed academy.

To the left of the "Shrine" is seated the *Rosh
Hak'neseth*, the President of the congregation;
behind his chair stands the *Chazan Hak'neseth*, the
beadle, to his right and left the officers of the congregation are seated, at their feet sit the elders.

These three groups sit with their faces towards
the congregation, while the congregation faces
the shrine.   In the center of this capacious inter-

†Exodus xxv: 31-36.

ior is the "Almemor," or the "Bimah," a spacious elevated platform of magnificent design. A balustrade encircles this platform, whose balusters, as well as those of the graceful stairways that lead up to the platform on both sides, are of delicate alabaster columns. On this "Bimah" is the Reader's desk, and the Rabbi's pulpit, placed there, that the vast audience may have the opportunity of advantageous hearing.

From the ceiling great chandeliers are suspended, which shed a shower of light upon the host of worshipers, and streaming through the inexpressibly beautiful stained-glass windows, the synagogue, that towers high above the city of Cordova, sheds its benign rays of holiness and peace and good will over the city and all its people.

The floor of the vestibule is composed of marble, mosaics and glazed tiles, so joined as to form various complicated patterns of surpassing beauty. The floor of the synagogue is covered with embroidered Persian carpets.

Though the seats are filled, and the officers are in their respective places—

'No sound is uttered—but a deep
And solemn harmony pervades."

Verily, the Hebrews understand the essence of worship well. There is in every prayerful soul that indefinable yearning and longing after the infinite, after the highest and the sublimest that can give eloquent utterance in deep silence only. The soul may stammer forth its wants and its thanks, but its deepest, innermost feelings never.

Therefore have the jews established the custom
that the service of expression shall ever be preceded by the still more sacred service of silent
meditation.

The strange surroundings, and the wondrous
sights, have so completely taken hold of our mind
that it cannot find that calm repose so necessary
for silent devotion, and so, while the others are
lost in meditations our mind, continues its observations.

Two men rivet our attention. The one is
Chasdai ben Isaac, one of those awe-and-respect-
commanding and love-and-confidence-inspiring
appearances we meet with but rarely in life. His
features present an embodiment of three distinct
races. His high and square forehead, his deep-
set eye, his aquiline nose, his prominent chin,
indicative of profound wisdom, of capacities to
command and of great will power; these bespeak
the Palestinian Hebrew. The grace and come-
liness of the figure bespeak the Moor. His tall,
majestic form, full of life and vigor, bespeak the
European Visigoth.

No less attractive is the person of Rabbi *Moses
Ben Chanoch.* There is something strange and
fascinating in his intelligent countenance. Some
strange, sweet melancholy seems to hover about
his eyes. The lines of his face fall into an expression of mild suffering, of endurance swetened and
sustained by holiness and resignation to God's
will. He seems to be more deeply lost in meditation than any of the rest. Now and then his
forehead wrinkles, and his lips quiver, as if in

pain, and his teeth close, as if suppressing a cry of anguish.

Is the great and learned and pious Rabbi, revered wherever a jewish heart beats, whether in Asia or in Africa or in Europe, through whom the light of Eastern learning, which, by the dispersion of the illustrious teachers, and by the final closing of the great schools, seemed to have been extinguished forever, suddenly rose again in the West in renewed and undiminished splendor, is he really lost in pious meditations? We have our suspicious, and may God pardon us if we suspect him wrongfully.

"There are moments when silence, prolonged and unbroken,
More expressive may be than all words ever spoken,
It is when the heart has an instinct of what
In the heart of another is passing." *

It may be, he recalls the day of his departure from Sura, in company with his young and beautiful wife, and his little son, and three other young and eminent rabbis, Rabbi *Sahamaria ben Elchanan*, Rabbi *Chuschiel* and Rabbi *Nathan ben Isaac Kohen*, for the purpose of raising funds for the academy at Sura, which was then in its last throes. He is recalling, perhaps, the harrowing scene when they were taken captive along the Italian coast by the Spanish-Moorish pirate, Admiral *Ibn Rumachis*. His quivering lips and wrinkled brow and his suppressed cry of anguish betray his thinking of the evil designs which the pirate admiral carried in his foul heart against his young and beautiful wife; how she, the pious

---

* Lucile, Pt. II., Canto I., St. 20

and innocent, preferring death to infamy, had asked him, concealing the motive: whether there is resurrection for those who perish in the sea; and how he, unsuspecting, answered in the affirmative, basing it upon Psalm lxviii: 23. "The Lord said, I will bring again from Bashon, *I will bring again from the depths of the sea,*" how she, no sooner had the answer been given, plunged into the sea, and the raging billows swallowed his young and beautiful wife, the mother of his young and only child.

Hence, his wrinkled brow and quivering lip and melancholy expression on the blessed Sabbath eve. No illuminated home awaits him. No wife that has cheerfully labored all day long to prepare for the festive reception of the Sabbath. No wife to greet him with her cheery smile, and with her wise and pure and holy converse to dispel the cares and worries of the week. No mother to press his child against her love-beating bosom and call him, too, "My own sweet child."

His thoughts continue in their wandering. He recalls the day when he was sold as slave to Cordova; how he was ransomed by the jewish community, though his quality and learning were unknown; how he entered, one day, the school for Talmud studies, over which Rabbi *Nathan,* "Dayan" of the jews of Cordova, presided; how he, ashamed of his costume of sackcloth, seated himself in a corner, at a respectful distance from the disciples; how he, aroused, at last, by the false decisions of the ignorant Rabbi Nathan, forgetting in his excitement his humble state, and his costume of sackcloth, ventured to correct, with becoming modesty, the decisions rendered; how all eyes had turned towards the poor slave; how, to draw forth his learning, Rabbi Nathan entered into a debate with him, in which he evinced such profound scholarship that Rabbi Nathan exclaimed with enthusiastic admiration.

"I am no longer Head of this School—Yon slave in sackcloth is my master, and I his disciple."

His mind continues in its reveries. He recalls how he had been installed by acclamation as Head of the jewish community; how he had gained the favor of Chasdai and of the Caliph; how his great school was founded and is flourishing now, and is the most famous in the Jewish literary world.

His face becomes more and more placid. He recognizes the finger of God in his fate. His capture, and that of his three colleagues, he sees now, has been providential. They had been destined to carry the knowledge from the schools of Babylon to Africa and Europe. His colleagues had fared equally as well. Rabbi *Sahamaria ben Elchanan* had been sold as a slave to Alexandria, where he, too, was ransomed by the jewish community, and later he also established a flourishing school at *"Misr"* (Kahira). Rabbi *Chuschiel* met with the same fate. He was sold to *Kairuan*, on the coast of Africa, and there he, too, opened a school. Rabbi *Nathan ben Isaac Kohen* was sold to *Narbonne*, France, and, as if fate had so ordered it, he too opened a flourishing school at that place. He would have continued his reveries had not the "*Sh'liach Hazibur*' aroused him, who leaves his side, and mounting the "*Almemor*," takes his place at his desk. The services are to begin, and so we, too, must cease our observations, and unite with our co-religionists in their joyous and reverential greeting of the weekly Sabbath, the blessed Day of Rest.

CHAPTER VII.

A SABBATH EVE IN CORDOVA

(CONTINUED.)

THE EVENING SERVICE.—A BEAUTIFUL CUSTOM IN ISRAEL.—HONORED
WITH AN INVITATION TO CHASDAI'S HOUSE.—ILLUMINATED
STREETS.—THE TWO ANGELS.—AN IDEAL SABBATH IN
AN IDEAL HOME.—THE PRAISE OF THE VIRTUOUS
WOMAN.—A FATHER'S BLESSING.—PRESENTED
TO THE LADIES.—THE EVENING MEAL.
THE JEWISH KINGDOM OF THE
KHOZARS.

The "*Sh'liach Hazibur*," (Reader) has taken
his position before the lecturn upon the "*Bimah.*"
From a voluminous parchment folio he chants the
beautiful and joyous Psalms xcv, xcix, cii, in that
fascinating musical *recitative*, peculiar to Hebrew
liturgy, so joyous and yet so holy, so gay and
yet so reverential, so intensely sacred, so religiously elevating as to lift the worshiper on its
mighty pinions, gently, form week-day life into
the higher and purer Sabbath realm.

The "Reader" and the congregation sing
alternate verses. What a grand chorus of human
voices! What majestic strains wing their heaven-
ward flight! How sublime a music to hear these

hundreds of men entune their sacred anthems to
God.   Sweet is the sound of the melting harp
and of the warbling lute, but sweeter than both
is the music that rises from the warm human
breast.   Touching are the strains of the night-
ingale and the lark, but sublimest and most
touching of all is the sacred music that rises from
the innermost depths of the strong and masculine
heart.   Such

> "Music religious heat inspires,
> It wakes the soul and lifts it high
> And wings it with sublime desires,
> And fits it to bespeak the Deity."

To hear a man weep, to see his strong bosom
melt in tears and his great grief express itself in
eloquent sobs, breaks another's heart, to hear
him sing with fervor and devotion the praises of
God, gives the strongest stay to the human soul.
When men sincerely sing religious songs their
hearts speak.   When we hear the Elders in front,
yon saintly patriarchs, laureled with the silver
crown of three and four and five score years,
mingle their voices with those of the young in
the religious songs, we know such songs raise
their weary souls above mortal weakness, soften
their pain to ease, stay the ruthless hand of fell
disease, and force death itself to sheathe, yet
awhile, his unsparing scythe, and our lips involuntarily breathe forth the benediction: Praised
be Thou, O God, who hast blessed us with the
gift of song.

The congregation rises and the "Reader"
chants aloud the *Borchu*, the appeal to the con-

gregation "to worship God, the Worship deserving," to which they answer: "Yea, we will
worship God, for deserving of praise is He, now
and evermore."

They resume their seats and continue their
prayers. They render thanks for the genial hour
of twilight, which bids the weary laborer cease,
and takes him to his peaceful home, and rewards
him there with shelter and with rest. They
render thanks for the revealed truths and doctrines conducive to moral good and human excellence, and sincerely they pray, that, as long as
in their thoughts and deeds God's word is their
law, and that law their light, they may never be
without his fatherly care. Again they rise; amidst
awe-inspiring solemnity, the "Reader" chants
Israel's great creed: *"Hear, O Israel, the Eternal,
our God is One,"* to which the worshipers respond
in one grand chorus: "Praised be the name of
His glorious kingdom forever and aye."

Silent, but fervent, devotion ensues. They
express their deathless faith in the God of their
fathers, in Him who sustains life, supports the
falling, heals the sick, takes to himself the souls
of the departed, crowns the week with the blessed
Sabbath day, and they conclude praying that
God may keep their tongues from evil, their lips
from uttering deceit, and arm them with meekness
against ill will, that he may impart humility in
their soul and faith in their heart; that He may
be their support when grief silences their voice
and comfort them when woe bends their spirit,
that truth may illuminate their path and wisdom

be their guide; that He may frustrate every evil
device and turn to goodness the hearts of those
who devise them.

The ''Reader" breaks the silence by taking a
goblet of wine, and with it, as the symbol of joy,
he entunes the *Kiddush*, the consecration of the
Sabbath as a day of rest and joy and spiritual
elevation.

The mourners and those who commemorate
the anniversary of the death of some dear departed, rise now and recite the *Kaddish*, the
"Mourner's Prayer," by which they utter even in
their painful trials, their pious submission to God's
will and to His superior wisdom.

How sublime this mourner's service! How
consoling to those who mourn and weep, to those
who have mourned and wept, and how instructive
to those who are destined to mourn and weep!
It is as fraught with goodly lessons for those
whom the hand of death has spared as for those
who have been afflicted. It is more potent to
move the heart than are the most fervent prayers,
more eloquent than the most stirring discourses.
Would you have your family life the sweetest,
the purest, the most blessed, while it lasts, then
go to the synagogue, hear the Mourner's *Kaddish*,
and think how that heart must feel that has seen
one of its links, neglected while living, go down
into the lonely grave, there, where all the acts of
charity and kindness, where the choicest of flowers
and most expensive of monuments can cheer the
silent sleeper no more. Would you have help to
overcome jealousy and hatred, contempt and evil

thoughts and evil deeds, go to the synagogue, hear the solemn "Kaddish," learn from it that there is a time when regret and repentance come too late to be heard, a time when sobbing and wailing can not pierce the clods. Would you moderate your ambitions and check your appetites, would you see the frailty of the mortal, would you keep your heartstrings vibrating in sympathy with suffering humanity, would you have a clear conception of the ends and aims of life, would you keep your conscience pure, then go to the synagogue, see the mourners rise, and from their sighs and tears learn the lesson that for the proud and the humble, the high and the low, the learned and the ignorant, the rich and the poor, the tyrant and the slave, the king and the servant there is but one common goal, death equalizes them all, his scythe knows no caste, no creed, no name, no fame, no title and no rank.

But we have strayed from the living to the dead, from the joyous to the sorrowful. Let us return to the service.

Again the congregation rises and solemnly they read the "Olenu," the concluding prayer, in which they express their fervent hope to behold soon the splendor of God's majesty, such as will call unbelief to vanish from the earth, will banish wickedness forever, will lead all mortals to recognize and worship the One and Only God, and bring on that glorious day when all men will live together in unity and brotherly peace, and the spirit of enlightenment will reign supreme over all.

Another joyous Sabbath hymn and the services are concluded.

In the vestibule, in the meantime, a number of strangers, showing by their appearance and costume to belong to different countries and to different stations of life, had gathered. They awaited there the conclusion of the services to be invited home for the Sabbath meal, for it is considered a sin in Israel if a brother in faith, be he rich or poor, friend or stranger, passes, or is permitted to pass, the joyous Sabbath Eve by himself, alone and forsaken, and it is regarded an act of piety to grace the festive board of the Sabbath meal with the presence of strangers. And so the company of these strangers is pressingly solicited, and the invitation is cheerfully accepted. Moses ben Chanoch, the Rabbi, and jacob ben Eleasar, the special messenger, who had on that day returned from the jewish kingdom of the Khozars, and we, who were cordially greeted after we were presented by our friend Dunash ben Labrat, are the guests of the distinguished "Nasi."

Through whatever streets we pass, the houses inhabited by Jews vie in their brightness with the brilliant illumination of the streets. A bright and cheery home on the Sabbath Eve is a law unto the Jew. "From the house that is cheerfully illuminated on the Sabbath great minds will issue" *spoke the Talmud, and it said still more: "When the Israelite leaves the synagogue for his home, on the Sabbath Eve, an Angel of Good and an Angel of Evil accompany him. If, upon

---

Talmud Babli Sabbath 23b.

entering his home, he finds the table spread, the Sabbath lamp lighted, and his wife and children attired in festive garments, ready to receive him, and in unison with him to bless the Holy Day of Rest, the Good Angel sweetly speaks: "Thy next Sabbath, and all the Sabbaths shall be as bright and as happy as this. Peace unto this dwelling forever," to which the Angel of Evil says a reluctant "Amen." But if no preparations have been made to greet the Sabbath, if light, and song, and thanksgiving do not cheer the inmates of the house, then the Angel of Evil exultingly speaks: May thy next Sabbath and all thy Sabbaths be as this. Gloom, misery, dissension, unhappiness unto this dwelling forever," to which the Angel of Good, bathed in tears, stammers forth a reluctant "Amen." *

Upon entering the palatial residence, the very atmosphere breathes holiness and peace. Scarcely has Chasdai ben Isaac crossed his threshhold, when, in accordance with the established custom in Israel, in a joyous but sacred melody, in which his mother, and wife, and children join, they sing the salute to the Sabbath angels at the domestic hearth, repeating each verse three times. Thus it runs:

"Peace unto you, ye angels of God, ye high messenger from the King of Kings, praised be He."

"May your coming be in peace, ye angels of God, ye high messengers from the King of Kings, praised be He."

* Talmud Babli Sabbath 119b.

"Bless us with peace, ye angels of God, ye high messengers from the King of Kings, praised be He."

"Let your parting be in peace, ye angels of God, ye high messengers from the King of Kings, praised be He."

Then fondly taking his mother by his right hand and his wife by his left, and leading them both lovingly to the center of the room beneath the radiant glow of the hallowed Sabbath lamp, he sings the last twenty-one verses of the last chapter of the Book of Proverbs, that noblest of all noble tributes to the virtuous woman, which reads as follows: "The heart of the husband of the virtuous woman doth safely trust in her, so that he shall not want for gain. She will do him good and not harm, all the days of her life. She seeketh wool, and flax, and workethwith diligent hands. She is like the merchant ships; she bringeth her food from afar. She riseth also while it is yet night, and giveth meat to her household, and the day's work to her maidens. She considereth a field and buyeth it. With her fruit of her hands she planteth a vineyard. She girdeth her loins with strength and maketh strong her arms. She sees that her trading yields good profit; her lamp is kept burning by night. She layeth her hands on the spindle, and her hands hold the distaff. She stretcheth out her hands to the poor, yea, she reacheth out her hands to the needy. She is not afraid of the snow for her household, for all her children are clothed with scarlet wool. She maketh herself robes, her clothing is silk and purple. Her husband is known in the gates, when he sitteth among the elders of the land. She maketh fine linen and selleth it, and delivers girdles unto the merchants. Strength and honor are her clothing, and she smiles at days to come. She openeth her mouth with wisdom, and in her tongue is the law of kindness. She looketh well to the ordering of her household, and eateth not the bread of idleness. Her sons rise up and praise her, her husband also, and he extols her. Many daughters have done virtuously, but thou excelleth them all. Gracefulness is deceitful, and beauty is vain, but a woman that feareth the Lord, she shall be praised. Give her the honor that the fruits of her hands deserve; her works are the praise of all in the gates."

The scene of that happy group, Chasdai, the learned and sagacious minister of the Moorish realm, facing his wife and mother, and encircled by his children, singing this glorious tribute to the virtuous women—a weekly tribute that has done much toward establishing the beauty and grandeur of the jewish family life—the wife, whose beautiful form and features and grace express nobility of character and godliness within, as she lowers her black and musing eyes, as her bosom heaves with tender emotion, and her countenance is mantled with the scarlet hue of innocence at her husband's enumeration of her praises; the queenly mother, majestic and tall ¸as her son, and in her beauty a rival to his beautiful wife, as she holds her eye with speaking pride upon her distinguished son; that scene is for the artist's brush and for the sculptor's chisel. It is too beautiful, too pathetic, too sublime for the feeble tongue or pen.

The children crowd to their father, and kissing them fondly, he lays his hands in blessing upon them. Verily, blessed is the head upon which parents' hands lie in blessing, and blessed are the parents' hands that lie in blessing upon a child's head. We know now whence to trace the cause of Chasdai's greatness and nobility of mind and excellence of character. That happy home life reveals to us the secret of his success. Here is the perennial fountain whence he quaffs daily the sweet draughts of moral goodness and human excellence. Here is that earthly paradise where kindness and good will, and peace, love, joy, reverence, mingle and produce continuous ecstatic bliss.

We are presented to the ladies and a hearty welcome is written on their countenance. We are no stranger to them, for Dunash ben Labrat has kindly announced us in advance, and they are pleased with our presence, for they, too, are longing to hear of the entrance of the Jews into Europe, especially of the entrance into Spain. We are shown our places at the festive board. A servant pours water on our hands from a basin and ewer. Chasdai rises, and filling a goblet with wine, he repeats, in melodious strains, the "Kiddush," the ceremony we had already seen in the synagogue, the consecration of the Sabbath as a day of rest and joy and spiritual elevation within the sacred precints of the home. From beneath a beautifully embroidered cloth he takes the Sabbath loaf, recites the benediction, and breaking it, gives a piece thereof to every diner. And now the meal begins, spiced with excellent conversation, in which the women enter as lively as the men, and more than once their profound knowledge and brilliancy of mind and subtle wit exact from us expressions of admiration. The chief topic of the conversation is concerning the Jewish kingdom of the Khozars, from whom Jacob ben Eleazar had brought the anxiously-awaited news that morning. What we gather from this conversation is this:

West of the Caspian Sea is a powerful kingdom, named "Khozar," before the strength of which the Persian monarchy trembles, and whose favor and alliance is courted by the Greek Empire. Its original inhabitants were a Turcoman tribe, who had gradually abandoned their nomadic habits and maintained considerable commerce. Their capitol, Bilangiar, is situated at the mouth of the Volga, and a line of cities stretches across from thence to the Don. Merchants of all religions, Christians, Mohammedans and Jews, were freely admitted, and their superior intelligence over his more barbarous subjects had induced one of their kings, Bulan (740 A. C.), to embrace the religion of the Jews. His choice between the conflicting claims of Christianity, Mohammedanism and Judaism was decided in this manner: He examined the different teachers apart. He asked the Christians if Judaism was not better than Mohammedanism.   To which the Christians replied affirmatively.   He asked the Mohammedan teachers if Judaism was not better than Christianity.   To which they, too, replied in the affirmative.   Both deciding in favor of Judaism, the king embraced the faith of Moses, and induced learned Jewish teachers to settle in his domains.   A belief in Judaism is the necessary condition on the accession to the throne.   The most liberal toleration of all other forms of faith prevails.   But of this Jewish kingdom nothing was known in Spain till Chasdai learned of its existence through the ambassadors of the Byzantian emperor.   Chasdai, to assure himself fully of the sovereignty possessed by his brethren, had sent Jacob ben Eleazar as a messenger to them, with a letter to their king, which concluded thus: "Were I sure of the existence of this kingdom I would throw aside all my present honors and positions, and, hastening to it, would throw myself at the feet of a Jewish king and feast my heart and eyes at the sight of his might and splendor."   That very day had brought the eagerly looked-for letter from the present King of the Khozars, Chagan Joseph, giving the above information, and concluding thus: "I, too, am desirous of knowing thee and of profiting by thy wisdom.   Could my desire be gratified, and could I speak to thee face to face, thou wouldst be to me as a father, and I thy son, and into thy hand would I intrust the government of my kingdom."

The meal was finished and grace was said. Dunash ben Labrat, mindful of the promise he

had made to Abdallah ben Xamri to bring him
whenever Chasdai would relate to us the history
of the entrance of the Jews into Spain, had come
with his Moorish colleague, and they are announced. Chasdai leads the way to the library,
and we follow.

CHAPTER VIII.

THE ENTRANCE OF THE JEWS INTO EUROPE.

CHASDAI'S LIBRARY.—HIS ACCOUNT OF THE ENTRANCE OF THE JEWS
INTO EUROPE.—THE DESTRUCTION OF JERUSALEM.—A TERRIBLE
CARNAGE.—ISRAEL CEASES AS A NATION.—THE DIASPORE.
THE DAUGHTER-RELIGIONS THRIVE UPON THE SUFFER
INGS THEY INFLICT UPON THE MOTHER-RELIGION.
THE INDESTRUCTIBILITY OF ISRAEL.—HUMILATED
BUT NOT FORSAKEN.

When we were comfortably seated in the magnificent library of Chasdai ben Isaac, which was
furnished luxuriantly, and with an eye to ease
and comfort, and stocked with thousands of
parchment folios, which stood row upon row,
from floor to ceiling, in beautifully arched and
decorated alcoves, along the walls of the spacious
library hall, our host, Chasdai ben Isaac, began:

"My friends, you asked for an account of 'The
Entrance of the Jews into Europe.' The task you
honor me with is not an easy one. Upon these
shelves stand side by side the best that has been
written upon History, Theology and Science, the
classics, old and new, in their various tongues,
both in prose and poetry, all that has been writ-

ten for and against the religions of Mohammedanism and Christianity and Judaism, and yet
among these thousands of volumes you will search
in vain for historic traces of the movements of the
Hebrew people since their exile from their native
soil. Nay, more, you may even look through
the vast library of the Caliph, than which exists
at present (950 A. C.) none greater upon the face
of the earth, and still you will find naught upon
this subject. You may consult the most renowned
scholars of our age and meet with no better result.

You marvel why so little is known of the
History of the Jews during the period that extends
from the *Diaspore* (70 A. C.) to the time of the
conquests of the Arab-Moors of Spain, yet you
will cease to marvel when you reflect upon the
degradations, persecutions, cruelties, sufferings
heaped upon them, when you remember that
histories are never written of those who are considered outcasts, pariahs, moral lepers, the
accursed by God and man, and the so degraded
and execrated, the so persecuted and so barbar-
ously treated are not over-zealous to rejoice their
scourgers by flaunting the history of their suffering in their face. What I know of that period is
little, and that little have I secured only after
much labor and diligent research.

Insatiable Rome, she who had made the world
her slave, in whose realm the sun ne'er set, and
who, to vaunt of so vast a power, had killed in
cold blood, and for no offense at all, fully as
many as she ever claimed among the living had
stretched at last her cruel hand against Pales-

tine, and the "separate" and "peculiar" and sacred land became a heathen heritage. Jerusalem, the Holy City, lay in ruins. Smoking embers marked the site where stood the Temple of Temples, and the glory of Israel fell, and fell forever, and Israel ceased, and ceased forever, as a nation among the nations of the earth.

Rome enacted a carnage within the holy city, the like of which her inhuman legions, with all their multitudinous and murderous experience, had never seen before. What the famine had left the sword consumed, and what escaped the sword fell a prey to the flames, and what remained, after streams of human blood had quenched the flames, dropped dead beneath the pestilence, and they, that had defied all these grim allies of cruel death, were driven into an open space, the tallest and most handsome were reserved to grace the triumphal march of *Titus*, to be dragged along the streets of Rome with a halter around their neck, and to be executed after the eyes and ears of the Romans had had their fill of the conquered's sufferings; of the rest, all above seventeen years of age were sold to distant countries, to the most cruel servitude, or they were distributed among the provinces to give sport to the people by their gladiatorial combats, fighting for their lives against hungry and ferocious beasts.

One million one hundred and ten thousand Jews perished during this siege; ninety-seven thousand were driven in chains as slaves to distant lands. The old and feeble, and the young and helpless who were spared, not from mercy, but because the Romans for once, weary of their slaughter, and sickened from the loathsome sight and insufferable stench that arose from the heaps of unburied,putrid bodies, were forced to retreat. This pitiable remnant was compelled to take the staff of exile.

Forth they went from their native soil to roam the wide world over. Everywhere homeless, friendless, despised, trodden down, hunted down by man and beast, tortured, an object of derision, a shadow of their former greatness.

And when occasionally a ray of tolerance found its way to these outcast people,. and under the spell of its genial warmth the degraded dog was metamorphosed again into a human being, and the Jewish mind awoke again into life, and the Jew, strengthened and rejuvenated and encouraged, dared to enter again into the arena of useful activity, that single ray was at once recalled by priests, who were more cunning and contriving than humane and godly, for only upon the suffering of the mother-religion could the daug1ter-religion expect to exist. It was feared that the prosperity of Judaism would prove the absurdity of Christianity's and Islam's claims and prophecies. If the Jews are permitted to prosper and flourish and follow their religion, and that religion is shown to be full of life and vigor, what reason for existence have the daughter-religions? Success and prosperity must accompany only that religion which the masses are to accept and follow, and for which superiority is claimed over the others. Such was their sophistical and self-interested

reasoning, and so they afflicted and tortured the
Jews, denied them every human right, and then
kindly and magnanimously credited God with
their own wickedness, claiming that God visited
these punishments upon the Jews for·their rejec-
tion of Christ or Mohammed.   Hence, the uninterrupted persecutions and sufferings of the Jews.

But God had not withdrawn his guiding hand
from His Chosen People.   He had cast them
down, but he forsook them not.   Never before
had they been so nigh unto extinction, and still
they despaired not. With David they said: 'Yea,
though I walk through the valley of the shadow
of death, I fear no evil, for thou art with me; thy
rod and thy staff shall comfort me.' * They lost
not their faith in God and in their divine mission.
They doubted not that there was a meaning to
their sudden change of fortune.   They believed
that as each seed when sown must endure darkness and suffer decay before it can multiply its
kind a hundredfold, so had God scattered the
children of Israel as seeds among the nations of
the earth, and subjected them to threats and sufferings that the number of true believers might
increase a thousandtold.   They regarded it a
special distinction to be chosen by God to spread
monotheism and civilization among the children
of men.†

"This strong faith in the superior wisdom of
God's doing was the elixir that preserved them
during their indescribable sufferings.   This it was
that established unconsciously a bond of union

---

* Ps. xxiii. 4.   † Talmud Babli, Pessachim 87 b.

among them, scattered though they were, and whithersoever they went, however near to or however far from the land where once stood the cradle of their nation, their temple and palaces, where ruled and sang and spoke their princes and bards and inspired orators of deathless fame, however removed from this dearly beloved center, one past and one future, one hope and one aim, characterized them all and planted within them the seeds of indestructibility.

What wonder then that soon after this terrible national calamity, a disaster from which no other people on the face of the earth could have possibly survived, we hear of large Jewish communities in Asia, Africa and Europe ? Some of these were established even before the dissolution of the Jewish kingdom. At the time of Titus numerous Jewish communities existed in the countries bordering on the Euphrates and the Tigris, in Asia Minor on the north coast of Africa, in Greece and in Italy. The Jewish community in Rome was large and influential long before the reign of Titus, having been brought thither as slaves by *Pompey*, after his conquest of Jerusalem. After the terrible siege of Jerusalem, crowds of exiles wandered to them and swelled their number, and these destitute exiles must have diminished the community's opulence and respectability and popularity, for before the *Diaspore* Latin authors speak of them as a wealthy and respected community ; after this period, the notices of them by *Juvenal* and *Martial* are contemptuous, and imply that many of them were in the lowest state of penury, the outcasts of society.

Whatever city in Asia Minor and Greece the Apostle Paul enters he seems to find a synagogue. In some of these cities the Jews seem to have flourished ; in most of them, however, they were proscribed as an odious people, and were objects of hatred and abhorrence. The rule seemed to be, in localities were Christianity predominated the Jews suffered ; where the Heathens were in power the Jewish communities flourished.

In Italy they were permitted, with few exceptions, to live in peace. Even though *Theoderic* wrote : " Why should we give them peace in this life, when God will not give them peace in the life to come ? " and even though *Cassiodorus* piously bestowed upon them the flattering appellations of "scorpions, wild asses, dogs,"etc., it never came to very serious persecutions, and the valiant defense of *Naples* by the Jews against the great *Belisarius*, for which History gives them their deserved credit, clearly shows how the Jew can be patriotic for his adopted fatherland.

Concerning the Jews in Western Europe, we have no knowledge before the second century. When the Franks and Burgundians conquered the Roman colonies in Gaul, the Jews, who had been brought thither as slaves, were classed by the victors, as Romans, and shared equal fate with them. They were permitted to follow agricultural pursuits and trades. Their own ships furrowed the ocean. Jewish physicians were sought by the princes of the Church and of the Realm. As soldiers they distinguished themselves in the warfare between Clovis and Theoderic. Their religions practices were not interfered with, the Jew was everywhere respected by the heathen.

But the sun of their prosperity was extinguished when the heathen kings adopted Christianity. With the change of their religion came a change of heart ; the heart that was formerly full of love toward the Jew, turned into stone.   The clergy dictated, and the kings and the people obeyed with the sword, and the Jews bled and suffered and perished by the thousands, or were dragged under tortures to baptism into the alone-saving and all-loving church.

So much for the early history of the Jews in France.   We now come to the history of the Jews in Spain.   That theme is vast.   It demands a chapter for itself.

CHAPTER IX.

THE ENTRANCE OF THE JEWS INTO SPAIN.

JEWS SETTLE IN SPAIN DURING THE REIGN OF KING SOLOMON.—JEWISH
AGRICULTURAL SKILL MAKES ANDALUSIA THE GARDEN SPOT OF
EUROPE.—PROSPERITY THE GREAT CRIME OF THE JEWS.—THE
BEGINNING OF JEWISH PERSECUTIONS IN EUROPE.—CRUEL
LAWS.—VENGEANCE.—JEWS CONSPIRE WITH COUNT
JULIAN AND MOORS AGAINST SPAIN.—VICTORY.
MOORISH APPRECIATION OF THE SERVICES
OF THE JEWS.

The week had passed. It was Sabbath Eve
once more. Again we assembled in the library
hall of Chasdai ben Isaac to listen to the narrative
of "The Entrance of the Jews into Spain."
When all were gathered Chasdai began and
spoke as follows: History is more communica-
tive about the entrance of the Jews into Spain
than she is about their entrance into any of the
other West European countries. The Bible gives
us sufficient basis to build upon the fairly reliable
theory that as early as the time of King Solomon
(1,000 B. C.) the Iberian peninsula was known
to the Israelites, that considerable traffic was
carried on between them and the autochtones of

the Southwestern corner of Europe, and that a settlement of a Jewish colony within the sunny lands of Andalusia may have taken place then. We have a tradition which tells us, that when in the early days of the Christian era the Jews of Spain were attacked for having crucified Jesus, they claimed that neither they nor their fathers had any share in the crucifixion, that they were the descendants of Jews who lived in Spain long before the time of Christ, and produced a grave-stone upon which was inscribed · "This is the grave of Adonirams, the servant of Solomon the king, who came hither to collect the tribute for the king."

We know that when the Romans became complete masters of Spain in the second century B. C. they found a considerable number of Israelites domiciled there. About 60 A. C. the Jewish community of Spain must have been strong and influential enough to make the coming of the Apostle Paul among them necessary.*

Crowds of exiles wandered westward and swelled their number after the terrible siege of Jerusalem by Titus, and in addition 80,000 slaves are said to have been transferred thither and sold as slaves and speedily ransomed by their more fortunate brethren. Historic sources are agreed that these Jewish inhabitants of Spain by their passionate fondness for agricultural pursuits, a passion which they had brought along from the Holy Land, soon made Andalusia the garden spot of Europe, and by their industry, frugality, skill in traffic and intellectual powers, they became

* Romans xv:28.

the pillars of the country's prosperity and acquired great wealth and distinction.

It could not have been otherwise. In habits, aims and ambitions there was an organic difference between the Jews and their warlike fellow citizens. The Romans, as well as the Visigoths, were wedded to military life. Every other calling or pursuit was degrading in their eyes. Trading or tilling the soil was in their eyes only befitting the slave. The uncertainty of their future, their roaming life, their habit of living from plunder, developed in them traits that were just the opposite to those of the Jews. The Jew hated war. His love for home was intense. His industry and frugality, his religious life and his love of study, were proverbial, and so in proportion as the others increased in brutality and ignorance, in poverty and moral corruption, the Jews reached the heights of prosperity, morality and intellect.

That prosperity, however, proved to be their curse. It is a mistake to believe that the greatest crime of the Jews was their faith ; it was their prosperity. Idlers and spendthrifts have never yet been thrilled with ecstatic delight at another's prosperity, and never is their venom more poisonous and their wrath more bitter than when the Jew is unfortunate enough to be fortunate. In Spain, as elsewhere, a mighty power of soldiers, and monks, and priests, and dependants, all unproductive laborers, stood arrayed against the handful of Jews, the only productive laborers of the realm, and the battle cry was not the Jews' money, but the Jews' "soul." There was great

diplomacy in this battle cry.   They knew of the
intensity of the Jew's faith in his religion.   They
knew how he was wedded to the traditions and
hopes of his race.   They knew that he would
cheerfully part with all his treasures rather than
sacrifice an iota of his belief.   They knew that
the industrial, and economical, and intellectual,
and peace-and home-loving traits of the Jew were
so deeply rooted, that he would at once begin
anew to acquire again, perhaps for the same end,
all that had been cruelly torn from him, just as
the bees, nothing daunted by the theft of their
painfully hoarded wealth, will start anew to fill the
hive.   And so, whenever they had need of the
money of the Jews, and that need was, alas, a
frequent one, they became all at once painfully
concerned about the Jewish soul, and its final fate,
and they never failed to relieve the Jews of their
treasures, even if they failed in the saving of their
souls.

Spain took the lead in Jewish persecutions and
maintained its odious distinction for centuries.
Henceforth there is no lack of historic material
concerning the Jews in Spain.   But, alas! until
the time of the conquest of Spain by the Moors,
it is not a history of achievement, it is a history of
suffering—a martyrology.   That martyrology
began with the Third Council of Toledo (589 A. C.)
at which Recaredo presented his abjuration of
Arianism and was anointed as the first Catholic
monarch of Spain.   At that council laws were
passed, of which the spirit may be comprehended
from the following preamble and titles :

"Laws concerning the promulgation and rati-
fication of statutes against Jewish wickedness, and
for the general extirpation of Jewish errors.
That the Jews may not celebrate the Passover
according to their usage ; that the Jews may not
contract marriage according to their own customs;
that the Jews may not practice the Abrahamitic
rite ; that the Jews bring no actions against Christians ; that the Jews be not permitted to bear witness against Christians."

The Jews knew what was wanted ; they paid
a large sum of money, and the laws remained in-
operative till Recaredo's successor, Sisebuto, ascended the throne. This king entered into a
league with Emperor Heraclius, with the pious
determination of " extirpating the dangerous race
throughout the world," and so he issued a law
which gave the Jews a year's time to decide whether they would confess Christ and be
baptized, or be shaved and scourged, their property confiscated, and themselves forced to leave
the country.*

Ninety thousand are said to have submitted to
baptism, but with them the enforced Christian
rite was but a mask for their secret Jewish belief
and practices. And they had ample cause for re-
gretting their religious weakness, for baptism did
not secure them from new indignities and humilia-
tion. They were despised for their apostacy, and
their property was taken from them as if they

---

*"Confessar la region cristian y bautizarse, o ser decalvados, azotados,
lanzados del reino y conficados sus bienes." Codex Visigothorum xii.,
t t iii.

had not complied with the king's edict.   Thousands upon thousands fled to the northern coasts of Africa, and with them fled the prosperity from the Gothic kingdom.

Having once discovered so excellent a source for satisfying their greed for money, they had no intention of letting such golden opportunities escape them.   A few years had passed, and the baptized Jews, true to their industrial and economical habits, had hoarded up some wealth with which they might buy life from the infuriated mob, and so the Fourth Council met at Toledo, in the year 633, and enacted the cruel requirement that the children of those, who had accepted Christianity, should be torn, forever, from their parent's heart, to be educated by Christians in the Christian faith.   The Sixth Council enacted a law, that every king on his accession shall take an oath, that he will execute all the laws against the Jews, and will issue others equally as severe. Another law enacted the punishment of death upon Christians, who should embrace Judaism, or commit "the monstrous and unutterable crime of pursuing an execrable commerce with the ungodly."   The Ninth Council decreed, that all baptized Jews were bound to appear in the church, not only on Christian, but also on Jewish holidays, lest, while they outwardly profess Christianity, they should practice secretly Judaism.

The Twelfth Council, of Toledo, 681, far surpassed its predecessors in the cruelties of its enactments.   The preamble complained that "the crafty Jews had eluded all former laws," and then

decreed that hereafter 100 lashes would be inflicted upon the naked body, and after that, the of-
fender would be put in chains, banished, and his
property confiscated for any of the following of-
fences : For rejecting the sacrament of the
Lord's Supper, for not bringing children or servants or dependants to baptism, for observing the
Passover, the New Moon, the Feast of Taber
nacles, for violating the Christian Sabbath, or the
great festivals of the church. The circumcision
of a child brought additional tortures, upon the
father mutilation, upon the mother the loss of
her nose. No marriage was hereafter to be con-
tracted, without solemn obligation that both would
become Christians. All subjects of the kingdom
who harbored, assisted or concealed the flight of a
Jew, were to be scourged, and have their property confiscated. The Jew who read or allowed his children to read books written against
Christianity was to suffer 100 lashes ; on the
second offense the lashes were to be repeated,
with banishment and confiscation. No Jew was
to hold any office by which he might have authority over Christians.

I shall spare you a recital of the numerous
other cruel laws enacted, and the account of
the terrible sufferings endured. The land re-
echoed the piteous groans and lamentations of
the lashed and scourged. Their wealth purchased but temporary immunity and exemption.

"Certainly the heroism of the defenders of every
other creed fades into insignificance before this
martyr people, who confronted all the evils that

the fiercest fanaticism could devise, enduring obloquy and spoliation and the violation of the dearest ties, and the infliction of the most hideous sufferings, rather than abandon their faith. For these were no ascetic monks, dead to all the hopes and passions of life, but were men who appreciated intensely the worldly advantages they relinqished, and whose affections had become all the more lively on account of the narrow circle in which they were confined. Enthusiasm and the strange phenomena of ecstasy, which have exercised so large an influence in the history of persecution, which have nerved so many martyrs with superhuman courage, and have deadened or destroyed the anguish of so many fearful tortures, were here almost unknown. Persecution came to the Jewish nation in its most horrible forms, yet surrounded by every circumstance of petty annoyance that could destroy its grandeur, and it continued for centuries their abiding portion. But above all this the genius of that wonderful people rose supreme. While those around them were grovelling in the darkness of besotted ignorance ; while juggling miracles and lying relics were the themes on which almost all Europe was expatiating ; while the intellect of Christendom, enthralled by countless superstitions, had sunk into a deadly torpor, in which all love of enquiry and all search for truth were abandoned, the Jews were still pursuing the path of knowelege, amassing learning, and stimulating progress with the same unflinching constancy that they manifested in their faith."*

*Lecky's Rationialism in Europe, (pages 270–271) vol. 2, chap. 6, and

The enemy succeeded in impoverishing the
Jew, and in stifling his energies and efforts for
the good of the country, but failed ignominiously
in their effort to inspire him with a love for
Christianity, which perhaps was never sincerely
wanted, and, if wanted, the means chosen to
secure the end were not such that are crowned
with success. The degraded and tortured Jew
was filled with a bitter hatred against Christianity,
and with a burning longing for revenge.

And vengeance came. God had heard the wail-
ings and seen the sufferings of the people that
never was born to die. The Gothic kingdom of
Spain was to suffer bitterly for its terrible crimes
and the Jew was to be rewarded a thousand-
fold for the sufferings he had endured for his
religion's sake. Weaker and weaker became
that kingdom which the Jews had made in former years the pride of Europe. It was beset by
foes within and by foes without. The tyranny of
the church and of the throne had instigated dissa-
tisfaction among the grandees of the state, and
the insult of Roderick, the king, to Florinda, the
young and beautiful daughter of Count Ilyan
aroused this bravest of Spanish warriors and

---

also the following from Prescott's Ferdinand and Isabella (p. 192), vol. 1:
"Under the Visigothic empire the Jews multiplied exceedingly in the
country, and were permitted to acquire considerable power and wealth.
But no sooner had their Arian masters embraced the orthodox faith,
than they began to testify their zeal by pouring on the Jews the most
pitiless storm of persecution. One of their laws alone condemned the
whole race to slavery : and Montesquieu remarks, without much exaggeration, that to the Gothic code may be traced all the maxims of the modern
Inquisition, the monks of the fifteenth century only copying, in reference
to the Israelites, the bishops of the seventh."

numerous powerful friends of his into open rebellion.

Nearer and nearer drew the Arab-Moors.
They reached the Northwestern point of Africa,
where the Jews, who had fled and who had been
banished thither, and who had risen there
to power and influence, greeted them with a
hearty welcome. The martial sound of the Moslem
hosts made as pleasant music to their ears as to
the insulted father and his wrath-inspired followers. Both parties conspired with the Moorish
chief, Amir Musa Ibn Nosseyr, for the invasion
of Spain. Musa grasped eagerly at this ardently
wished-for opportunity. He dispatched his valiant
warrior Tarik, with 12,000 men across the narrow
strait that separated Africa from Europe, and
Islam from Christianity. Roderik met him at the
banks of the Guadalete with an army eight times
as large, and that day was the last Spain beheld
him and his army. On that day Christianity
ceased to rule within the land of Spain, and as its
power sank, there dawned once more the sun of
prosperity unto Israel.

The Moors did not forget the valuable services
of the Jews. The early hatred against them in
Arabia, for refusing to accept the creed of
Mohammed, had long since been converted into
tolerance and good will. Unlike the religion of
Christianity, which started as the religion of love
and soon became the religion ot the sword,
Islamism began as the religion ol the sword but
soon become the religion of love. Political and
religious freedom and social recognition was

granted to the Jew throughout the caliphate, and from that day unto this the two Oriental people have lived in peace side by side upon the Oecidental soil, vieing with each other in their noble efforts to restore unto Spain her original beauty and prosperity, and to make her in culture and art and intelligence the mistress of Europe. We, sons of Israel, have labored hard and zealously in this noble contest, but with all our efforts our rival has passed beyond us, and humbly we cede the palm of victory to the Arab-Moors."

Here Chasdai ben Isaac ceased. He had spoken of the sufferings of the Jews with such perceptible anguish, he had related the part which the Jews took in the conquest of Spain with such vivid animation, and referred to the prosperity of the Jews under Moorish sway, and to Moorish tolerance and intellectual greatness, with such touching pathos that when he paused, a deep impressive silence ensued. At length Abdallah ben Xamri, the Moorish poet laureate to Caliph Abder Rahman III., arose, advanced towards Chasdai, and bowing low, thus he spoke:

'Your modesty must not bridle my tongue. I would appear an ingrate to my people should it become known that I listened in silence to your last remarks The Arab-Moors forgot not their benefactors, nor are they so boastful as to arrogate to themselves, or allow others to bestow upon them a superiority which is unmerited.

Within our heart of hearts we treasure the services which your people have rendered. We owe the Hebrew people much more than your modesty, noble Chasdai, has suffered you to claim. You opened the portals of Spain unto us, and to you alone belongs the credit of turning Spain once again into a paradise, for a hundred years of uninterrupted warfare under the banner of Islam, had unfitted us for agricultural and mechanical and intellectual and artistic pursuits. You sowed the seeds of our prosperity. We sat at the feet of your masters, and if we have proven ourselves apt scholars, we bear testimony to the excellency of your teachers. Far be it from us to claim superiority over our honored rival. In the arts and sciences and philosophies your people hold distinguished places. Your theologians have given us many a problem which the wisest among us have failed to solve. In the purity of your home and social life, and in your industries you serve the world as models. In poetry I should never venture to compete for supremacy with friend Dunash ben Labrat and Menachem ben Saruk. In diplomacy, where lives the man who can equal you in intellect and sagacity, to whom else do we owe our political greatness than to you, Chasdai ben Isaac, the Jewish minister of our beloved Caliph Abder Rahman III."

CHAPTER X.

THEIR POSITION IN MEDICAL SCIENCE.

THE FIFTEENTH CENTURY.—A CHANGE IN THE FORTUNES OF THE JEWS
AND MOORS.—AN EXAMINATION INTO THEIR GREAT ACHIEVEMENTS.
THEIR SKILL IN MEDICAL SCIENCE —MIRACLE CURE BY CHRIS-
TIAN CLERGY —JEWISH BODY PHYSICIANS HIGHLY PRIZED
AND MUCH SOUGHT. — PROMINENT MEDICAL SCHOOLS AND
EMINENT PHYSICIANS —RASHI —IBN EZRA —IBN TBBON.—
MAIMONIDES —AVENZOAR AVACENNA

We have witnessed the rise of Islam. We accompanied the Arab on his march of conquest.
Breathlessly we stood upon the banks of the
Guadalete and awaited the issue of a battle upon
which the destiny of nations depended. We
followed the triumphal processions of the Arab-
Moors into Spain, and our eyes and hearts never
ceased rejoicing over the manifold beauties and
wonders which Moorish skill spread o'er fair
Andalusia, and our tongues ne'er tired speaking
of the manifold blessings which Moorish social
and domestic and political life and religious tolerance showered lavishly not only upon their own
generation, but upon all the generations that have
been ever since.

And there was another picture, not so beautiful, but far more instructive; not so cheering, but fuller of pathos. Tearfully we witnessed the siege of Jerusalem and its unparalleled massacre. Heartbroken we followed the despised and spurned and abused, the friendless and homeless Jew, in his vain efforts to find a spot where he might rest his weary head in peace. Our hearts leaped for joy when we beheld the followers of Mohammed—not the followers of the founder of the religion of love—not only restore to the Jew human rights unjustly torn from him, but also offer him the hand of brotherhood. When we parted last we left the Jew and Moor busily engaged in making fair Andalusia, in culture and art and intelligence, the mistress of the world. Then all was peace and joy and sunshine.

We have returned. Five centuries have passed since our last visit. We are now at the end of the fifteenth century. A mighty change has taken place. Peace has turned to war, joy to sorrow, sunshine to darkness. Culture wears the crown of thorns. Art is dragged through the mire. Science is fettered hand and foot. Religious liberty sends forth piteous shrieks from the flames and smoke of the auto-da-fe. Enlightened Europe weeps and trembles. We ask Mercy: "Why weepest thou?" And she sobs forth the name: "Cardinal Ximenes" We ask Art the same question, and she stammers forth: "The Church." Science answers: "The Inquisition." Religious Liberty utters between its death throes the name: "Torquemada." Enlightened Europe weeps and trembles, because the vast storehouses of learning, which Moorish and Jewish intelligence had built up, are about to be consigned to the flames, and the builders themselves are to be extirpated from the soil, upon which they have lived nigh unto eight centuries, and which their own diligent toil has made the wonder of Europe.

"Haste ye," the Spirit of knowledge calleth unto us, "the furnaces are heated, the death-pyres are awaiting impatiently their martyrs, the ships are ready in the harbor to carry off, and give abundance of water to all such who refused the few drops of the water of salvation, the massive gates of the Inquisition dungeons are open, and the instruments of torture are eager for their cruel and inhuman work of death. Haste ye, the moments are precious, gather the knowledge for which you have come, as speedily as you can; tarry, and not a trace nor a record will remain of this most wondrous and fruitful era of Europe's intellectual advance."

Let us heed the warning, and hasten to our task. We had come prepared for a detailed account, but now we must content ourselves with a mere synoptical sketch of the progress made by the Arabs and Jews in literature, art, philosophy and in the mathematical and physical and applied sciences, during the same era when the rest of Europe was yet lying in comparative darkness and barbarism.

A feeling of awe comes over us as we approach our task. We cannot but feel that in dealing with the Arab and Jew in Europe, the period that

extends from the beginning of the eighth to the
end of the fifteenth century, we are dealing with
a divine agency, sent into Europe to rekindle and
keep alive the sacred fire of intelligence, which,
prior to their coming, had been extinguished by
the church and by barbarian conquerors.   At
this era they are the sole depositories of learning.
The second and third chapters of this narrative
have acquainted us with the terrible stifling mist
of ignorance and its concomitants, fanaticism and
cruelty and corruption and intense suffering,
which hovered over Europe at the time when the
people of the Orient had entered it, and began
their intellectual unfolding.

In the East those centers of learning that had
not yet passed away were rapidly declining. Antioch, Alexandria, Bagdad, Damascus, Jerusalem,
these cities which in their day had made the light
of the East more luminous with their light, had
drawn in their rays and sent them forth no more.
But the Jew and Arab had wandered into Europe
before this intellectual decline, and there they
fanned the spark of knowledge they had brought
with them into such a brilliant and active life, that
its light still illumines our mind, and its genial
warmth still cheers our heart.   The Jew and the
Moor have made Europe their everlasting debtor
for their services in bridging the yawning chasm
which separates ancient from modern culture.
With them, most of that ancient knowledge,
for which mankind had toiled diligently and un-
tiringly for thousands of years, would have been
lost, and lost forever, and modern knowledge,

would have been compelled to begin again at the very alphabet, and we to-day might have been some 2,000 or 3,000 years behind. Without their untiring efforts to disperse the poisonous mists, and force their light upon the people, even at the expense of much suffering, the darkest, and most slothful period of European annals which was co-eval with the highest Jewish and Moorish intelligence before that intelligence made itself felt in Europe, might have still surrounded us to-day.

But this is not the time for reflection nor laudation. Hark! Already the doeful knell is tolling, and the people are thronging the public square, and the clergy are chanting hymns of victory and imprecatory formula, and the *autos-da-fe* are piled up high and dry, and the condemned are impatient, for they long for death, they pray to be released, at last, from the insufferable tortures of the Inquisition, and so we must hasten to our task of recording upon History's pages the wonderful strides the Jews and Moors did make in science and literature and philosophy, before flame and sword and rack and expulsion, silence their voice and obliterate their works forever.

We shall consider their intellectual labors in the order of their importance and service to humankind, and for that reason we shall begin with a hasty review of their progress in medical science. In this branch the Jew was without peer. He excelled the Moor, because the restrictions which Ismalism imposed upon the follower of the Koran, such as prohibitions against dissecting man or animal, did not trammel him. And he eclipsed the Christian, for the Church held medical science accursed, branded and condemned the physician as an atheist, and zealously propagated the doctrines that cures must be wrought by relics of martyrs and bones of saints; by prayer and intercession; that each region of the body was under special spiritual charge, the first joint of the right thumb being in care of God the father, the second under that of the blessed Virgin, and so on to the other parts. For each disease there was a saint. A man with sore eyes must invoke St. Clara. St. Anthony is a sure cure for other inflammations, St. Pernel delivers from ague. In all cases, cured or not, the clergy constituted themselves as the self-appointed agents for collecting the fees for the saints, and as long as this spiritual method of curring disease formed one of their most productive sources of gain, they took great care that no other mode of treatment should excel theirs. Hence their attitude against physicians, and their frequent council decrees, making it a crime punishable with death for a Jewish physician to attend a Christain patient, and for a Christain patient to seek recourse to a Jewish physician, instead of to the shrines and altars of the saints.* But for all that, Jewish physicians, and Jewish medical schools flourished, and found their prohibited profession very profitable among the Christians, especially among kings, and popes, and princes, and bishops, among the very men, who passed the sentence of death for crimes which they were the first to perpetrate.

---

*Council of Beziers, 1246 A C.; Council of Alby, 1254; Faculty of Paris, 1301.

In the tenth and eleventh and twelfth centuries, nearly all the physicians in Europe were Jews. Later, the Moors joined them, but only for a short time, and then the Jews again became the sole champions of medical science. There was not a man of power or prominence who had not his own Jewish body physician, and these body physicians constituted a power, for besides holding the lives of potentates in their hand, they combined with their professional skill, all the learning of the age, a profound knowledge of theology, mathematics, astronomy, philosophy, music, law, statesmanship, poetry lexicography, criticism, and of other branches.

In naming them and their schools and their works we must give honorable mention to the Jewish physicians of France. Out of the Spanish peninsula there had came across the Pyrenees an intellectual influence which found a warm reception by the Jews of France. To verify this, of schools, we need but name the famous medical school at Narbonne under the presidency of Rabbi Abbu, and the flourishing school at Arles, and the most famous of them all, the college of Montpellier, with the great Profatius as regent of the faculty, as distinguished in medicine as he was eminent in astronomy ; and of the distinguished Jewish physician of France, we need but name Rabbi Solomon ben Isaac, (1040-1105) better known under the abbreviation · "Rashi," the greatest French physician of the eleventh century, unrivaled in his age for his instructions in great surgical operations, as the Cæsarean section ; nor must we forget the learned Ibn Tibbon, (1160-1230) who emphasized the necessity of a close study of botany for medical purposes, and of carefully cultivating the art of preparing drugs.

The scope of this discourse will not permit us to name all of the distinguished Jewish physicians of Spain, nor to enumerate their works nor to dwell upon their merits. From the many we shall select the name of Ibn Ezra, (1093-1107) the polyhistor of his age. His chief work is a treatise on practical and theoretical medicine, entitled, " Book of Proofs."

But greater than Ibn Ezra, both as a physician and a philosopher, is Moses Maimonides, (1135-1204), honored by his countrymen with the titles · " The Doctor," " The Great Sage," " The Glory of the West," "The Light of the East, Second Only to Moses " He was the most famous of all living physicians of his time. He was coveted as body physician by the greatest potentates, and the justly celebrated Sultan Saladin considered himself honored and fortunate to secure him as his body physician. When Richard Cœur de Lion, King of England, fell sick, Moses Maimonides was summoned for consultation. His contributions to medical works are many. He wrote medical aphorisms derived from former Greek, Latin, Hebrew and Arabic sources ; an abridgment of Galen, a treatise on " Hemorrhoids," on " Poisons and Antidotes," on " Asthma," on " The Preservation of Health," on " The Bites of Venomous Animals," and other valuable works. *

---

* For details see, Graetz's Geschichte der Juden," volume 5 and 6,

We return to the Moors, and here, too. we are confronted by an abundance of medical literature. Over 300 distinguished medical writers are mentioned, and their works are voluminous. Chief among them stands Avenzora, Ibn Zohr, (beginning of the Twelfth century) physician, to the court of Seville. His famous work "Canon of Medicine," an encyclopaedia of medical knowledge, established for him a world wide reputation and became the medical authority for European universities for many centuries. Upwards of 100 other medical treaties are ascribed to him, some are tracts of a few pages. others are works extending through several volumes. Avicenna (Ibn Sina, 980-1037) occupies an honored place next to him. Chief among his works is his "Method of Preparing Medicine and Diet," "Treatment of Leprosy," and two works on "Fever," in which he continues the work begun a century before by the Jewish physician, Isaac ben Suleiman Israeli. The Moors themselves acknowledge that the Jews far surpass them in their knowledge of anatomy, physiology and hygiene, that from want of knowledge of the construction of the human body, their surgery is necessarily crude. Their great fame, however, rests, and will rest, upon their introduction of pharmacy, their therapeutical use of drugs, their making chemistry, the handmaid of medical treatment. Pharmacopoeia dates from this period.   The

Moors of Spain, opened the first apothecary shops, and many of the names and many of the medicines still used, have come down to us from their period.*   We must content ourselves with this brief review (more the scope of this work will not permit,) of "The Position of the Jew and the Moor in Medical Science."

* For full information consult " History of Medicine," by J. F. Payne; " Geschichte der Arabischen Aertste und Naturforcher," by Wustenfeld.

CHAPTER XI.

IN THE SCIENCES.

MARVELOUS INTELLECTUAL SUPERIORITY OF MOORS AND JEWS — MOORS
EXCEL THE JEWS IN THE SCIENCES. — THEY INTRODUCE THE MATHE
MATICAL SCIENCES. — THEIR PROGRESS IN ASTRONOMY
ABSURD REFUTATIONS BY THE CHRISTIAN CLERGY.
THEIR RESEARCHES INTO CHEMISTRY, ZO-
OLOGY AND GEOLOGY. — THEY ANTICI-
PATE MODERN DISCOVERIES
EUROPE'S INGRATITUDE.

We turn next in our review of the intellectual
labors of the Moors and Jews in Spain, during
the period that extends from the beginning of
the eighth to the end of the fifteenth century, to
an examination of their position in the sciences.
The deplorably benighted state of contempo-
raneous Europe prepares us to expect little or
nothing in this noblest department of human
knowledge, and our surprise is therefore so much
the greater as we gaze upon, and ponder over,
the mighty strides made by the Moors and by the
Jews on the highways of science. The impetus
in this special branch seemed to have come from
the Arabs. The few words of Ali, the fourth
Arabian caliph : "Eminence in science is the

highest honor; he dies not who gives life to learning," seems to have taken as deep roots within
the minds of the Arabians, and to have yielded
far more precious fruits, than did the Koran the
vast volume of his distinguished father-in-law ;
Mohammed.

For centuries the Arab-Moors led the world in
this department. Here the Jews cannot lay claim
to rivalry ; they were collaborators, but nothing
more. In justice to the Jews, however, we shall
add, that there are some who differ from us in
our conclusion. Some give to the Jews an equal
rank with the Moors, others claim that the point
under discussion is still debatable. And we must
not treat their objection lightly. We must not
forget that in treating of these scientists of Spain,
we are dealing with men known under Arabic
names ; beyond a knowledge of their scientific
works we know little or nothing about them.
Concerning their religion, history maintains a
commendable silence; the Mohammedans preferring, at this period, the ink of science to
the blood of martyrs. Knowing of the scientific
scholars nothing more than that their works
are written in Arabic, and that their names
are Arabic, the canons of criticism will not permit us to conclude that a scientist who writes
in Arabic, and whose name is Arabic, is necessarily also a Mohammedan by faith. The records
give incontestable proof that many and many of
the distinguished Jewish scholars of that period
wrote in Arabic, and went under an Arabic name,
who, but for a chance article of work from their

pen upon a Hebrew subject, might have been
classed to-day as Arab-Moors by race and
Mohammedan by creed. Be this as it may.
That point will never be definitely settled, and as
long as a doubt remains, the Arab-Moors may
justly claim the benefit of the doubt, and the Jews
shall be the last to contest their claims of superiority in the sciences during the Middle Ages
over every other race or creed.

Entering upon our subject, and beginning at
the root of the tree of science, we make the pleasing discovery that to the Arab-Moors of Spain
belongs the honor of having been the first to
generally introduce in Europe, for scientific and
industrial and commercial purposes, the science
of arithmetic. Had they achieved nothing else,
the introduction of this most needful of all the
branches of mathematics alone, would have entitled them to a distinguised place among the
world's benefactors. That introduction was the
starting point of a new progress. Its use and
development made possible the higher mathematics and analytical mechanics and astronomy,
and every other science discovered since, and hail-
ed with delight. Little do we think to-day when
we pride ourselves on the startling achievements of our astronomers and meteorologists and
other scientists, when we speak of the miracles
they work in space and time, of the ascensions
they make to the remotest of the nebulæ, and of
their holding communion there with stars and
worlds and solar systems whose light has not yet
reached the earth, little do we think when we

speak of electricity obeying our every wish, and
of steam yoked in our service, and of the countless
other wonders of modern science, little do we
think that for all these blessings we are lastingly
indebted to the Arab-Moors, and to their assis-
tants, the Jews, for their faithful labors in mathe-
maties. Little do we think that we are pronounc-
ing Arabic words when we speak of the "zero"
or the "cipher", the "naught,"—that most important of all figures, upon which the most needful of all arithmetical contrivances is based—the
decimal system. And when we remember that
the prosperity and progress of every country in
Europe dates from the introduction of the Arabian
figures * and when we realize the clumsiness and
uselessness of the Hebrew and Greek and Latin
alphabet figures, in vogue in Europe before the
entrance of the Arab-Moors into Spain, and when
we try to work out a problem of multiplication,
say ninety-nine multiplied by ninety-nine, in accordance with the notation of the Arabic nine
digits and cipher, and then, in accordance with
the Roman alphabet figures, XCIX times XCIX,
then, perhaps, will we most readily give thank-
ful praise to those to whom Europe owes so
magnificent a boon—to those who, with so simple
an invention, opened the avenues of prosperity
and loosened the fetters that had shackled the
advance of science.

Encouraged by their success in arithmetic, they
turned towards a higher branch of mathematics

---

*In Germany and England not until the fifteenth century, and hence
their backwardness till then.

and gave to Europe the science of numbers and
quantity, and named it algebra ("al'jabara," to
bind parts together).   Whether, as some claim,
the Arab-Moors obtained their .knowledge of
algebra from their schools in Bagdad or Damascus, who, in their turn, had derived it from the
Hindoos, or whether, as others claim, the Jews,
in their diligent translations from the early Greek
geometricians into Arabic, must have come across,
and followed up the algebraic trace, which is supposed to exist in the treatise of Diaphantus (350
A. C.), or whether the Moorish claim be the true
one, that the honor of having invented algebra
belongs to one of their own mathematicians, who
flourished about the middle of the ninth century, to Mohammed ben Musa, or Moses, *
whoever the inventors be of this valuable branch
of mathematics, unanimity of opinion prevails
concerning one point, and that is, the Arab-Moors
and Jews first introduced algebra into Europe.
Still more Iben Musa (or Ben Moses) developed it
to the solution of quadratic equations, and Ibn
Ibrahim (Ben Abraham) to the solution of cubic
equations, Ibn Korrah (or Ben Korah) to the
application of algebra to geometry, laying thus
the foundation of analytical geometry.   Geometry led them to trigonometry, which they elevated
to a practical science by substituting sines for
chords and by establishing formulas and tables of
tangents and cotangents and secants and cose-

---

*A copy of this Arabic work is preserved in the Bodleian library
at Oxford, bearing a date of transcription corresponding to the year
1 342.

cants.   From trigonometry Al Baghadadi advanced to land surveying, and wrote on it a treatise so excellent, that by some it has been declared to be a copy of Euclid's lost work on that
subject.

The unbiased student, who searches diligently
among the achievements of the Moors and Jews,
will soon detect, not only a systematic contriv-
ance on the part of the literature of Europe to
put out of sight our obligations to them in science,
but a bold effort, wherever a chance presents
itself, to wrest their hard toil from them, and bestow it upon some one, who is not so unfortunate
as to be Saracen or Jew.   But "injustice founded
on religious rancor and national conceit cannot
be perpetuated forever."   The real truth can not
be much longer hidden, and if the chapters
of this volume have no other effect than
simply to do justice to the memory of those who
have toiled and who have suffered, that we
may enjoy, to-day,the blessings of our civilization,
we shall regard our labors amply rewarded.

We have digressed,   Let us return to our
theme.   They toiled for science sake, not for
fame.   They looked for none. When Spain itself,
indebted to them for all her blessings, repays so
miserably their faithful services, why should they
look to Europe for recognition? "High minds,"
it has been truly said, "are as little affected by such
unworthy returns for services, as the sun is by
those fogs which the earth throws up between
herself and his light."*

* T. Moores "Life of Sheridan," Vol. 2 Chap. iv.

And so, expecting no thanks, and working for none,they advanced. with their present achievements as stepping stones, to the study of astronomy. And marvelous, almost incredible, is their success in this department. They determine the altitude of celestial bodies by means of the astrolabe. They register all the stars in their heaven, giving to those of the first magnitudes the names they still bear on our celestial maps and globes, writing thus indelibly their impress upon the celestial heaven, though it be denied them in the literature of Europe. They give us the words "azimuth," "zenith," "nadir," "almanac," and others. They compute time by the oscillations of the pendulum, and determine the true length of the year. They discover the theory of the refraction of light and ascertain the curvilinear path of a ray of light through the air. They explain the horizontal sun and moon, and why we see those bodies before they have risen and after they have set. They measure the height of the atmosphere and determine it to be nearly fifty-eight and one half miles. They give the true theory of the twilight. and of the twinkling of the stars. They not only know the spheroidal form of the earth, but approximately its diameter and circumference. Averroes discovers the spots upon the sun. Kepler alludes honorably to the observations of Levi ben Gerson, and Copernicus to those of Profiat Duran, and Laplace accepts Ibn Musa's proof of the dimunition of the eccentricity. of the earth's orbit, and Ibn Junis' proof of the obliquity of the ecliptic. They invent the first pendulum clock.

They build the first observatory in Europe, the Giralda, (1196 A. C.) turned into a belfry after the expulsion of the Moors and Jews. They almost discover the laws of gravity, considering it terrestial, reserving it for Newton to teach that it is universal. Rabbi Isaac ben Sid prepares for Alphonso X., king of Castile, new astronomical tables, for which Alphonso takes the credit, names them the Alphonsine tables, and is modest enough to remark: "That if God had called him (the king) into His councils when He created the universe, things would have been in a better and simpler order."

The Church, in the meanwhile, does her best to refute the "ungodly scientific teachings" of the Moors and Jews. The argument of the "Sohar" that the earth revolves upon its own axis and around the sun (a Jewish teaching in the twelfth century, anticipating that of Copernicus), the shining lights of the church nail to the ground with clinchers from the Bible such as these· "The sun runneth about from one end of the heaven to the other," and "the foundations of the earth are so firmly fixed that they cannot be moved." The absurdity of the existence of the antipodes they prove to their full satisfaction in this manner: "It is impossible that any inhabitants exist on the opposite side of the earth, since no such race is recorded by Scriptures among the descendants of Adam." Again, "we are told by St. Paul that all men are made to live 'upon the face of the earth,' from which it clearly follows that they can not live upon more faces than one or upon

the back." Again, "how could men exist on the
other side of the earth, since on the day of judgment, being on the other side, they could not see
the Lord ascending through the air?"   Ergo, the
teachings of the Church alone are the true theories of this universe, "concerning which it is not
lawful for a Christian to doubt."

But the Moors and Jews treated with contempt
this puerile opposition, little thinking that the
Church of "Love unto all men" has stronger and
more convincing weapons than tongue and pen to
prove her points. They persevered in their path so
well begun. They turned to the physical sciences.
They originated chemistry.   They discovered
some of the most important reagents, such as the
nitric, sulphuric and hydrochloric acids, and alco-
hol, which still bears its Arabic name   They
knew the chemical affinities of gold, silver, cop-
per, iron, tin, lead and quicksilver.   They invented various apparatus for distillation, sublima-
tion, fusion, filtration, etc.   They constructed
tables of specific gravities.   In geology, Abu
Othman wrote a valuable work.   In zoology, the
following extract from a chapter of Avicenna
(Ibn Sinai or Ben Sinai) on the origin of the
mountains, which reads as if it were written by
one of the most advanced geologists of our
day, will best indicate the heights to which they
attained in this science.   "Mountains" said
Ibn Sina (980-1037), "may be due to two different causes.   Either they are upheavals of the
crust of the earth, such as might occur during a
violent earthquake, or they are the effects of

water, which, cutting for itself a new route, has denuded the valleys, the strata being of different kinds—some soft, some hard. The winds and waters disintegrate the one, but leave the other intact * * * That water has been the main cause of these facts is proved by the existence of fossil remains of aquatic and other animals on many mountains." *

But little has been cited here concerning the position of the Moors and Jews in the sciences. The field is too vast and the scope of this volume will not permit us to enter into greater details. He that would have fuller knowledge upon this theme let him peruse the following works, to which I am largely indebted for the facts stated above. "Geschichte der Arabischen Aerzte and Naturforscher," Wuestenfeld; "Conquest of Spain," "Book V.," by Coppe; "Eastern Caliphate," Stanislaus Guyard; "History of Algebra," Phillip Kelland; "History of

---

* Sometimes, not without surprise, we meet with ideas which we flatter ourselves have originated in our own times Thus our modern doctrines of evolution and development were taught in their schools. In fact, they carried them much farther than we are disposed to do, extending them even to inorganic and mineral things. The fundamental principle of alchemy was the natural process of development of metalline bodies. "When common people," says Al-Khazini, writing in the twelfth century, "hear from natural philosophers that gold is a body which has attained to perfection of maturity, to the goal of completeness, they firmly believe that it is something which has gradually come to that perfection by passing through the forms of all other metallic bodies, so that its gold nature was originally lead, afterward it became tin, then brass, then silver, and finally reached the devolopment of gold; not knowing that the natural philosophers mean, in saying this, only something like what they mean when they speak of man, and attribute to him a completness and equilibrium in nature and constitution—not that man was once a bull, and was changed into an ass, and afterward into a horse, and after that into an ape, and finally became a man."
— "*Conflict between Religion and Science,*" *by Draper, Chap. IV.*

Arithmetic," George McArthur; "Astronomy,'
R. A. Proctor; "The Intellectual Development of
Europe," Draper; "Conflict Between Religion and
Science," Draper; "Rationalism in Europe," Lecky.

Yet, even though our synoptical review has
been brief we have seen and heard enough to
understand fully why in the year 1492, and within the realm of Spain, Wisdom mourns and
Knowledge wails, and Science is broken-hearted
and Europe trembles. Anguish seizes upon our
soul at the thought, yet a little while, and all this
wondrous intellectual advance, so active and so
promising will be torn off the soil of Europe, root
and all, and darkness, cruel darkness, ignorance,
cruel ignorance, will ascend the throne once
more and usher into the scenes of life stagnation,
corruption, suffering, despair.

For science and for humanity's sake we venture to approach the princes of the realm and
prelates of the church and plead for mercy. "No!"
is the stern reply of Ferdinand and Isabella,
"Spain is polluted by the presence of the accursed
Moors and Jews." "Avaunt!" shouts Cardinal
Ximenes, "Catholicism is in danger where Moorish and Jewish brain is at work." "Mercy ye
ask for," fairly shrieks the Grand Inquisitor Torquemada, "the Church knows no mercy for the
Moorish and Jewish infidel dogs. Begone, or
their fate is yours."

We are not yet prepared for death. Our task
is not yet done. Many a Moorish and Jewish
achievement remains still to be spoken of, and so
we shall hasten our review, while yet we may
speak of their position in literature.

CHAPTER XII.

IN LITERATURE.

SPAIN'S PROSPERITY STIMULATES LITFRAIURE. —LAVISH PROVISIONS FOR
EDUCATION. —CALIPHS PATRONS OF LEARNING. —VASI LIBRARIES
EMBODYING THE KNOWLEDGE OF IHE DAY. —POETRY ESPEC
IALLY FOSTERED. —STORY-TEILING. —JEWISH AND
MOORISH POETRY CONTRASIED. —JEHUDA
HA LEVY. —CHARISI —GABIROL.
—MOSES BEN EZRA

When we turn to an examination of the position of the Jews and Moors of Spain in Literature,
and behold their progress in this department of
knowledge, we are not so much surprised as we
were when we surveyed the wondrous advance
both did make in the department of science, at a
time when the rest of Europe was still under the
spell of a mental torpor. The great epochs of
the world's literature have ever had their origin
during times of peace and prosperity. They may
continue into turbulent times, and even outlive
them, but never can they take root in them.
Such an age Spain and its people were enjoying
for many years under Moorish sway. The
Moors had ended their conquests, and for a while
the Jews enjoyed freedom from persecution.

Peace prevailed, and prosperity gladdened the
heart of man. ·Hills and dales yielded bountiful
harvests.   The rich mines of Spain brought to
light the treasures of the earth.   The long line of
coast was crowded with vessels, which restlessly
furrowed the oceans, exchanging the products of
Europe for the wealth of the Orient.   The commerce of the world centered in Spain ; there, too,
could be found its wealth.   The age was ripe for
literary activity.

The Jews were the first to open this epoch-
making era of European literature. The past
had shown that the Jewish mind needs no other
impetus for earnest intellectual toil than an age
of peace and prosperity, and the present marked
no departure from the general rule.   The Arab-
Moors, sharing the general characteristics of the
Jews, did not tarry long behind ; as the Jews were
mindful of the teachings of their sages, that the
crown of learning is the greatest of honors, so
did the Moors remember the words of the great
Caliph Al Mamum: "They are the elect of God,
they are His best and most useful servants, whose
lives are devoted to the improvement of their
rational faculties."   And so great was the literary
zeal of both these races that within comparatively
few years there arose a literature upon grammar,
lexicography, rhetoric, history, politics, biogra-
phy, translation, statistics, music, fiction, poetry,
law, ethics, theology. philosophy, much of which,
despite our boasting of to-day, not only need not
fear modern criticism, but is still authority.
And it endured for nearly eight centuries, ex-

ceeding in duration that of any other literature, ancient or modern, and even after it was crushed, it continued to emit a steady luster thróugh the clouds and darkness of succeeding centuries. Like a flood it overflowed the mountain barriers and went on widely irrigating the arid fields of Europe.

The provisions for education were abundant. To every mosque and synagogue a free school was attached. Endowed colleges dotted the Saracen Empire, in which free tuition was given to all who were eager for knowledge, and stipends were cheerfully furnished the indigent students. In addition to this, many of the caliphs distinguished themselves not only for their scholarly attainments, but also for their munificent patronage of learning. They assembled the eminent scholars of their times, both natives and foreigners, at their court making it the familiar resort of men of letters, establishling a precedent which the Medicis later turned to excellent use. Above all, they were intent upon the acquisition of extensive libraries. They invited illustrious foreigners to send them their works, and munificently recompensed them. No donation was so grateful to them as a book They employed agents in Egypt, Syria. Irak and Persia, for collecting and transcribing the rarest manuscripts; and their vessels returned freighted with cargoes more precious than the spices of the East. In this way they amassed magnificent collections— that of Alhakem Second amounted to 600.000 volumes. * Our own Harvard cannot reach half

*Prescott's "Ferdinand and Isabella," Book I, chap., 8, Conde's "History of Spain," II., chap., 88.

that number, even in the nineteenth century, and with the advantage of steam and printing press. Besides these royal libraries, seventy public libraries are named in Andalusia. The collections in the possession of individuals were sometimes very extensive. A private doctor refused the invitation of a sultan of Bokhara because the transportation of his books would have reqiured 400 camels·

The subjects upon which these thousands upon thousands of volumes treat are so manifold, and the authors so numerous—the department of history, for instance, according to an Arabian author cited by D'Herbelot, could boast of 1,300 writers—that even a synoptical review of them would need more space and time than the scope of these discourses will allow, and so we dismiss them with the s imple remark that such is their excellence, such the influence they exercised upon the literature of Europe that a careful perusal of the works still extant in the original or in translation will well repay the special student of any of the special branches of literature of which they treat.

The poetry of that period, however, refuses to be dismissed. She bids us halt, She, the queen of literature, is not accustomed to such slight. She was born to rule, she brooks no opposition, and so we pause. And after we have held sweet converse with her minstrel bards, and after we have perused a number of the almost countless volumes devoted to winged words of music and to poetic fancy, we regret not. that she made us pause. No longer do we think her boast an idle

one that Spain, during the period that extends
from the eighth to the fifteenth century, can show
a greater number of poets than all the other nations combined. We need not ask the reason
why. Any one acquainted with the extraordinary
richness of both the Hebrew and its kindred—
the Arabic language—their natural cadence,
which lends itself to verse, the ease which both
languages afford in passing from prose to poetry,
and with the bent of mind of both races, poetical,
delighting in figurative speech, in metaphor and
allegory and fable, in luxuriant imagery and fan-
ciful romance, any one acquainted with their
Oriental predeliction for the fairer sex, which
could only express itself in languishing idyls or
passionate lyric sonnets, any one knowing all
this, will not wonder at the vastness of the Jewish and Moorish poetic literature.

The Moors excelled in what was then known
as the art of "story telling." They had brought it
with them from the East and the enchanting moon-
light evenings of Andalusia, and the sequestered,
fairy-like gardens, with their shady cypress trees,
and their cascades, and their flowering shrubs,
and their bowers of roses, and their crypt-like
grottoes, all these tended to keep the love for their
art alive. With them "this story telling," both
in prose and poetry, took the place of theatrical
representation. Those of you familiar with one
of the many extant prose collections of stories
such as "The Arabian Nights," can readily form
an opinion of the great charm that branch of literature must have had in the original language
for the Moorish people.

Physicians often ordered "story telling" as a prescription for their patients, to mitigate. their sufferings, to calm their agitation and to give sleep after protracted insomnia, or to beguile the *ennui* of the grandees, or to recreate them after their fatigues. The "munshids" or "story tellers" found their vocation a very honored and a very profitable one, and they took great pains. to foster that art.

These stories and their lyric poetry exercised a potent influence over the literature of Southern and Western Europe. It can be traced in the reproduction of many stories as well as in the structure of the French "*fabliaux*" and "*chansons de geste*" of the "*jongleuers*" "*trouveres*" of the North; and is more particularly to be observed in "*le gai saber*"of Provencal troubadours. It extended into Italy, and is found in the charming stanzas of Ariosto, and in the "twice told tales" of Boccaccio's "Decameron."

In a word, the entire fiction and poety of Southern Europe, up to the Renaissance, owes as much to the Spanish-Arabians for matter and form, as it does to the Latin language.* Still more, when we remember that our English Chaucer borrowed the scheme of his "Canterbury Tales" from several of the stories of Boccaccio, and other Italian writers, and that other English writers imitated Chaucer in borrowing plots and subjects from Italy and France and Spain, we may well claim that the Arabian idea has penetrated into

*Fauriel's "Historie de la Poesie Provencal," chapter xiii.

the North, and left its profound impression upon English literature. *

But in the purer poetry, in touching tenderness of pathos, in sublimity of thought and majesty of diction, in those lofty flights where hope blends with sorrow, and with a religious fervor that is tempered by celestial sweetness and warmth of heart, here, the Jewish poets of Spain not only excel their Moorish rivals, but every poet before or since. Once more Israel's sons and daughters took their harps of Judea from off the mourning willows, and the Songs of Zion, the Glory of Israel, and the Praises of the Universal Father resounded again as sweet in the fairy land of Andalusia, as formerly upon the banks of the Jordan. They consecrated their Muse to the purest and holiest purposes. The epigram of Aben Esra, one of the immortal poets of this age, tells briefest and best the uses to which poetry lent itself among the various nations. He wrote:

"Among the Arabs in their fiery way,
The song doth breathe alone of loves sweet sway.
The Roman sings exultant of war's spoils.
Of battles, sieges and warriors toils.
In wit and spirit doth the Greek excel,
And India's bards of curious riddles tell,
But songs devoted to the Maker's praise,
The Jews alone among the nations raise."

We do not mean to convey by this, that the Jewish poets of Spain devoted themselves only and exclusively to the sacred song. *Jehuda Ha-*

* "Conquest of Spain," by Coppee, Book X.

Levi thus sings of love and wine as fiery as e'er did Moorish bard.*

LOVE-SONG.

"See'st thou o'er my shoulder falling
   Snake-like ringlets waving free?
Have no fear, for they are twisted
   To allure thee unto me."

Thus she spake, the gentle dove,
   Listen to thy plighted love:—
"Ah, how long I wait, until
   Sweetheart cometh back (she said)
Laying his caressing hand
   Underneath my burning head."

SEPARATION.

And so we twain must part! Oh linger yet,
   Let me still feed my glance upon thine eyes.
Forget not, love, the days of our delight,
   And I our nights of bliss shall ever prize
In dreams thy shadowy image I shall see,
   Oh even in my dream be kind to me!

Though I were dead, I none the less would hear
   Thy step, thy garment rustling on the sand.
And if thou waft me greetings from the grave,
   I shall drink deep the breath of that cold land.
Take thou my days, command this life of mine,
   If it can lengthen out the space of thine.

No voice I hear from lips death-pale and chill,
   Yet deep within my heart it echoes still.
My frame remains—my soul to thee yearns forth,
   A shadow I must tarry still on earth.
Back to the body dwelling here in pain,
   Return, my soul, make haste and come again!

Thus sings Moses ben Esra;

The shadow of the houses leave behind,
In the cool boscage of the grove reclined,
The wine of friendship from love's goblet drink,
And entertain with cheerful speech the mind.

Drink, friend! behold the dreary winter's gone,
The mantle of old age has time withdrawn,
The sunbeam glitters in the morning dew,
O'er hill and vale youth's bloom is surging on.

*This and the following selections are taken from Miss Emma Lazarus' translations in "Songs of a Semite."

Cup-bearer! quench with snow the goblet's fire,
Even as the wise man cools and stills his ire.
Look, when the jar is drained, upon the brim
The light foam melteth with the heart's desire.

Cup-bearer! bring anear the silver bowl,
And with the glowing gold fulfill the whole,
Unto the weak new vigor it imparts,
And without lance subdues the heroe's soul.

My love sways, dancing, like the myrtle-tree.
The masses of her curls disheveled see!
She kills me with her darts, intoxicates
My burning blood, and will not set me free.

Within the aromatic garden come,
And slowly in its shadows let us roam,
The foliage be the turban for our brows,
And the green branches o'er our heads a dome.

All pain thou with the goblet shalt assuage,
The wine-cup heals the sharpest pangs that rage,
Let others crave inheritance of wealth,
Joy be our portion and our heritage.

Drink in the the garden, friend, anigh the rose,
Richer than spice's breath the soft air blows.
If it should cease a little traitor then,
A zephyr light its secret would disclose.

Extracts from the Book of Tarshish or "Necklace of Pearls."

It was not for want of cause that the sedate greybeards of Cordova applied for legal aid to have the passionate love songs of *Abraham Ibn Sahal* prohibited, for there was not a youth or maiden in the city who could not repeat them by heart. And as to songs of war and wit and spirit, the "Makamen" of *Jehuda ben Salamo ben Alchofni*, better known as *"Charisi,"* gives ample proof to assure us that the Jews might have become dangerous rivals to the Roman and Greek writers had they fostered that phase of poetry as did these. Thus sings Charisi;

LOVE SONG OF CHARISI.

I.

The long-closed door, oh open it again, send me back
    once more my fawn that had fled.
On the day of our reunion, thou shalt rest by my side,
    there wilt thou shed over me the streams of thy
    delicious perfume.
Oh beautiful bride, what is the form of thy friend, that
    thou say to me, Release him, send him away?
He is the beautiful-eyed one of ruddy glorious aspect
    that is my friend, him do thou detain.

II.

Hail to thee, son of my friend, the ruddy, the bright
    colored one! Hail to thee whose temples are like
    a pomegranate.
Hasten to the refuge of thy sister, and protect the son
    of Isaiah against the troops of the Ammonites.
What art thou, O Beauty, that thou shouldst inspire
    love? that thy voice should ring like the voices of
    the bells upon the priestly garments?
The hour wherein thou desirest my love, I shall hasten
    to meet thee. Softly will I drop beside thee like
    the dew upon Hermon.

And as to the curious riddles which India's
bards did tell, let us translate one or two, from
Jehuda Ha-Levi to show that even into this field
of poetic fancy the Jewish mind did wander, and it
plucked there fruit as choice as India's bards did
ever pluck.   Ha-Levi asks, Who solves this:

Eye it has and yet is blind,
Of service it is to human kind;
Raiment it makes, both large and small,
And still itself is bare of all.

(Answer: "The Needle.")

Or this:

> Would true friendship ye maintain
> Hither come and learn it;
> What us would part we cut in twain,
> While we remain uninjured.
> (Answer: "The two knives of a pair of scissors.")

As to their skill in reflective and descriptive poetry, let the following specimens show·

NIGHT-THOUGHTS.

> Will night already spread her wings and weave
> Her dusky robes about the day's bright form,
> Boldly the sun's fair countenance displacing,
> And swathe it with her shadow in broad day?
> So a green wreath of mist enrings the moon,
> Till envious clouds do quite encompass her.
> No wind! and yet the slender stem is stirred,
> With faint, slight motion as from inward tremor
> Mine eyes are full of grief—who sees me, asks,
> "Oh wherefore dost thou cling unto the ground?"
> My friends discourse with sweet and soothing words·
> They all are vain, they glide above my head.
> I fain would check my tears; would fain enlarge
> Unto infinity, my heart—in vain!
> Grief presses hard my breast, therefore my tears
> Have scarcely dried, ere they again spring forth.
> For these are streams, no furnace heat may quench,
> Nebuchadnezzar's flames may dry them not.
> What is the pleasure of the day for me,
> If, in its crucible, I must renew
> Incessantly the pangs of purifying?
> Up, challenge, wrestle and o'ercome! Be strong!
> The late grapes cover all the vine with fruit.
> I am not glad, though even the lion's pride
> Content itself upon the field's poor grass.
> My spirit sinks beneath the tide, soars not
> With fluttering seamews on the moist, soft strand
> I follow fortune not, where'er she lead.
> Lord o'er myself, I banish her, compel
> And though her clouds should rain no blessed dew,
> Though she withhold the crown, the heart's desire,
> Though all deceive, though honey change to gall,
> Still am I Lord, and will in freedom strive.

TO A DETRACTOR.

The Autumn promised, and he keeps
His word unto the meadow-rose.
The pure, bright lightnings herald Spring,
Serene and glad the fresh earth shows.
The rain has quenched her children's thirst,
Her cheeks, but now so cold and dry,
Are soft and fair, a laughing face;
With clouds of purple shines the sky,
Though filled with light, yet veiled with haze.
Hark! hark! the turtle's mocking note
Outsings the valley-pigeon's lays.
Her wings are gemmed, and from her throat,
When the clear sun gleams back again,
It seems to me as though she wore
About her neck a jeweled chain.
Say, wilt thou darken such a light,
Wilt drag the clouds from heaven's height?
Although thy heart with anger swell,
Yet firm as marble, mine doth dwell.
Therein no fear thy wrath begets,
It is not shaken by thy threats
Yea, hurl thy darts, thy weapons wield,
The strength of youth is still my shield.
My winged steed toward the heights doth bound,
The dust whirls upward from the ground;
My song is scanty, dost thou deem
Thine eloquence a mighty stream?
Only the blameless offering
Not the profusion man may bring,
Prevaileth with our Lord and King.
The long days out of minutes grow,
And out of months the years arise,
Wilt thou be master of the wise,
Then learn the hidden stream to know,
That from the inmost heart doth flow.

WINE AND GRIEF.

With heavy groans did I approach my friends.
Heavy as though the mountains I would move.
The flagon they were murdering; they poured
Into the cup, wild-eyed, the grape's red blood.
No they killed not, they breathed new life therein.
Then, too, in fiery rapture, burned my veins,

But soon the fumes had fled.   In vain, in vain!
Ye cannot fill the breach of the rent heart.
Ye crave a sensuous joy; ye strive in vain
To cheat with flames of passion, my despair.
So when the sinking sun draws near to night,
The sky's bright cheeks fade 'neath those tresses black.
Ye laugh—but silently the soul weeps on;
Ye cannot stifle her sincere lament.

DEFIANCE.

"Conquer the gloomy night of thy sorrow, for the
          morning greets thee with laughter.
Rise and clothe thyself with noble pride
Break loose from the tryanny of grief.
Thou standest alone among men,
Thy song is like pearl in beauty."
So spake my friend,   'Tis well!
The billows of the stormy sea which overwhelmed my
          soul,—
These I subdue;   I quake not
Before the bow and arrow of destiny.
I endured with patience when he deceitfully lied to me
With his treacherous smile.

Yea, boldly I defy Fate,
I cringe not to envious Fortune
I mock the towering floods.
My brave heart does not shrink
This heart of mine, that, albeit young in years,
Is none the less rich in deep, keen-eyed experience.

A DEGENERATE AGE.

Where is the man who has been tried and found strong
          and sound?
Where is the friend of reason and of knowledge?
I see only skeptics and weaklings.
I see only the prisoners in the durance of the senses.
And every fool and every spendthrift
Thinks himself as great a master as Aristotle.
Think'st thou that they have written poems,
Call'st thou that a Song?
I call it the cackling of the ravens.
The zeal of the prophet must free poesy
From the embrace of wanton youths.
My song I have inscribed on the forehead of Time,
They know it and hate it—for it is lofty.

TO THE WEST WIND.

Oh, West, how fragrant breathes thy gentle air,
Spikenard and aloes on thy pinions glide
Thou blow'st from spicy chambers, not from there
Where angry winds and tempests fierce abide.
As on a bird's wings thou dost waft me home,
Sweet as a bundle of rich myrrh to me.
And after thee yearn all the throngs that roam
And furrow with light keel the rolling sea.
Desert her not—our ship—bide with her oft,
When the day sinks and in the morning light.
Smooth thou the deeps and make the bil'ows soft,
Nor rest save at our goal, the sacred height.
Chide thou the East that chafes the raging flood,
And swells the towering surges wild and rude.
What can I do, the elements' poor slave?
Now do they hold me fast, now leave me free;
Cling to the Lord, my soul, for He will save,
Who caused the mountains and the winds to be.

(Extracts from the Book of Tarshish, or "Necklace of Pearls.")

Thou who art clothed in silk, who drawest on
Proudly thy raiment of fine linen spun,
Bethink thee of the day when thou alone
Shalt dwell at last beneath the marble stone.

Anigh the nest of adders thine abode,
With the earth-crawling serpent and the toad,
Trust in the Lord, He will sustain thee there,
And without fear thy soul shall rest with God.

If the world flatter thee with soft-voiced art,
Know 'tis a cunning witch who charms thy heart,
Whose habit is to wed man's soul with grief,
And those who are close-bound in love to part.

He who bestows his wealth upon the poor,
Has only lent it to the Lord, be sure—
Of what avail to clasp it with clenched hand?
It goes not with us to the grave obscure.

The voice of those who dwell within the tomb,
Who in corruption's house have made their home;
"Oh ye who wander o'er us still to-day,
When will ye come to share with us the gloom?"

How can'st thou ever of the world complain,
And murmuring, burden it with all thy pain?
Silence! thou art a traveler at inn,
A guest, who may but over night remain.

But with all their distinguished merits in these branches of poetic literature, they laid no claims to recognition, nor shall we claim it for them. Their aspiration was higher. Their lay was sacred. Their ideal of poetic grandeur was the writing and singing of majestic hymns, and they have given us a hymnology, a collection of pure and sacred songs, that has never yet been equalled. We know not what rational religious fervor is, we know not what real piety is, we know not what joyful ectasy is, nor what tearful and penitent tenderness means, we know not what trust in, and love of God is, we know not what it is to hear the heart speak to and of God, and the soul sing her Maker's praise, we know not what passionate devotion to, and deathless love for, Israel's cause, for the memory of her glorious past and for the hopes of her future is, we know not what all these are and mean, until we have read some of the hymns and sacred odes and elegies and meditations of the Jewish poets of Spain. Turn to your "Day of Atonement" services; read there the inexpressibly beautiful contributions to sacred poetic literature by Rabbi *Solomon ben Jehuda Gabirol*, or Rabbi *Joseph ben Ibn Abitur*, or Rabbi *Bechai ben Joseph*, or Rabbi *Moses ben Esra*, or the greatest of them all Rabbi *Jehuda ben Samuel Ha-Levi*, and answer it, where have you seen and where have you read or heard, anything that will bear comparison, with their religious poetry? Let us see the following from Gabirol:

MEDITATIONS.

Forget thine anguish,
Vexed heart, again,
Why should'st thou langui h,
With earthly pain?
The husk shall slumber,
Bedded in clay,
Silent and sombre,
Oblivion's prey!
But, Spirit immortal,
Thou at Death's portal,
Tremblest with fear.
If he caress thee,
Curse thee or bless thee,
Thou must draw near,
From him the worth of thy works to hear.

Why full of terror,
Compassed with error,
Trouble thy heart,
For thy mortal part?
The soul flies home—
The corpse is dumb.
Of all thou didst have,
Follows naught to the grave.
Thou fliest thy nest,
Swift as a bird to thy place of rest.

What avail grief and fasting,
Where nothing is lasting?
Pomp, domination,
Become tribulation.
In a health-giving draught,
A death-dealing shaft.
Wealth—an illusion,
Power—a lie,
Over all, dissolution
Creeps silent and sly.
Unto others remain
The goods thou didst gain
With infinite pain.

Life is a vine-branch;
A vintager, death.
He threatens and lowers
More near with each breath.
Then hasten, arise!
Seek God, oh my soul!

For time quickly flies,
Still far is the goal.
Vain heart praying dumbly,
Learn to prize humbly,
The meanest of fare.
Forget all thy sorrow,
Behold, Death is there!

Dove-like lamenting,
Be full of repenting,
Lift vision supernal
To raptures eternal.
On every occasion
Seek lasting salvation.
Pour out thy heart in weeping,
While others are sleeping
Pray to Him when all's still,
Performing His will.
And so shall the angel of peace be thy warden,
And guide thee at last to the heavenly garden.

HYMN.

Almighty! what is man?
But flesh and blood.
Like shadows flee his days,
He marks not how they vanish from his gaze.
Suddenly, he must die—
He droppeth, stunned, into nonentity.

Almighty! what is man?
A body frail and weak,
Full of deceit and lies,
Of vile hypocrisies.
Now like a flower blowing,
Now scorched by sunbeams glowing.
And wilt thou of his trespasses inquire?
How may he ever bear
Thine anger just, thy vengeance dire?
Punish him not, but spare,
For he is void of power and strength!

Almighty! what is man?
By filthy lust possessed.
Whirled in a round of lies,
Fond frenzy swells his breast.
The pure man sinks in mire and slime,
The noble shrinketh not from crime,
Wilt thou resent on him the charms of sin?

Like fading grass,
So shall he pass.
Like chaff that blows
Where the wind goes.
Then spare him, be thou merciful, O King,
Upon the dreaded day of reckoning!

Almighty! what is man?
The haughty son of time
Drinks deep of sin,
And feeds on crime
Seething like waves that roll,
Hot as a glowing coal.
And wilt thou punish him for sins inborn?
Lost and forlorn,
Then like the weakling he must fall,
Who some great hero strives withal.
Oh, spare him, therefore! let him win
Grace for his sin!

Almighty! what is man?
Spotted in guilty wise,
A stranger unto faith,
Whose tongue is stained with lies.
And shalt thou count his sins—so is he lost,
Uprooted by thy breath.
Like to a stream by tempest tossed,
His life falls from him like a cloak,
He passes into nothingness, like smoke.
Then spare him, punish m t, be kind, I pray,
To him who dwelleth in the dust, an image
          wrought in clay!

Almighty! what is man?
A withered bough!
When he is awestruck by approaching doom.
Like a dried blade of grass, so weak, so low,
The pleasure of his life is changed to gloom.
He crumbles like a garment spoiled with moth;
According to his sins wilt thou be wroth?
He melts like wax before the candle's breath,
Yea, like thin water, so he vanisheth,
Oh, spare him, therefore for thy gracious name,
And be not too evere upon his shame!

Almighty! what is man?
A faded leaf!
If thou dost weigh him in the balance—lo!
He disappears—a breath that thou dost blow.
His heart is ever filled
With lust of lies unstilled.

Wilt bear in mind in his crime
Unto all time?
He fades away like clouds sun-kissed,
Dissolves like mist.
Then spare him! let him love and mercy win,
According to thy grace, and not according to his sin!

Or this of *Moses ben Esra.*

IN THE NIGHT.

Unto the house of prayer my spirit yearns,
Unto the sources of her beings turns,
To where the sacred light of heaven burns,
She struggles thitherward by day and night.

The splendor of God's glory blinds her eyes,
Up without wings she soareth to the skies,
With silent aspiration seeks to rise,
In dusky evening and in darksome night.

To her the wonders of God's works appear,
She longs with fervor Him to draw anear,
The tidings of His glory reach her ear,
From morn to even, and from night to night.

The banner of thy grace did o'er me rest,
Yet was thy worship banished from my breast.
Almighty, thou didst seek me out and test
To try and to instruct me in the night.

I dare not idly on my pillow lie,
With winged feet to the shrine I fain would fly,
When chained by leaden slumbers heavily,
Men rest in imaged shadows, dreams of night.

Infatuate I trifled youth away,
In nothingness dreamed through my manhood's day.
Therefore my streaming tears I may not stay,
They are my meat and drink by day and night

In flesh imprisoned is the son of light,
This life is but a bridge when seen aright,
Rise in the silent hour and pray with might,
Awake and call upon thy God by night!

Hasten to cleanse thyself of sin, arise!
Follow Truth's path that leads unto the skies,
As swift as yesterday existence flies,
Brief even as a watch within the night.

Man enters life for trouble; all he has,
And all that he beholds, is pain, alas!
Like to a flower does he bloom and pass,
He fadeth like a vision of the night.

The surging floods of life around him roar,
Death feeds upon him, pity is no more,
To others all his riches he gives o'er,
And dieth in the middle hour of night.

Crushed by the burden of my sins I pray,
Oh, wherefore shunned I not the evil way?
Deep are my sighs, I weep the livelong day,
And wet my couch with tears night after night.

My spirit stirs, my streaming tears still run,
Like to the wild bird's notes my sorrows' tone,
In the hushed silence loud resounds my groan,
My soul arises moaning in the night.

Within her narrow cell oppressed with dread,
Bare of adornement and with grief-bowed head
Lamenting, many a tear her sad eyes shed,
She weeps with anguish in the gloomy night.

For tears my burden seem to lighten best,
Could I but weep my hearts blood, I might rest.
My spirit bows with mighty grief oppressed,
I utter forth my prayer within the night.

Youth's charm has like a fleeting shadow gone,
With eagle wings the hours of life have flown.
Alas! the time when pleasure I have known.
I may not now recall by day or night.

The haughty scorn pursues me of my foe,
Evil his thought, yet soft his speech and low.
Forget it not, But bear his purpose so
Forever in thy mind by day and night.

Observe a pious fast, be whole again,
Hasten to purge thy heart of every stain.
No more from prayer and penitence refrain,
But turn unto thy god by day and night.

He speaks : "My son, yea, I will send thee aid,
Bend thou thy steps to me, be not afraid.
No nearer friend than I am, hast thou made,
Possess thy soul in patience one more night."

Read the following stanzas culled from Ha-Levi's "Elegy on Zion" and ask yourselves, where is the sacred epic that will compare with it?

ON THE VOYAGE TO JERUSALEM

I.

My two-score years and ten are over,
  Never again shall youth be mine.
The years are ready-winged for flying,
  What crav'st thou still of feast and wine?
Wilt thou still court man's acclamation,
  Forgetting what the Lord hath said?
And forfeiting thy weal eternal,
  By thine own guilty heart misled?
Shalt thou have never done with folly,
  Still fresh and new must it arise?
Oh heed it not, heed not the senses,
  But follow God, be meek and wise;
Yea, profit by thy days remaining,
  They hurry swiftly to the goal.
Be zealous in the Lord's high service,
  And banish falsehood from thy soul
Use all thy strength, use all thy fervor,
  Defy thine own desires, awaken!
Be not afraid when seas are foaming,
  And earth to her foundations shaken.
Benumbed the hand then of the sailor,
  The captain's skill and power are lamed.
Gaily they sailed with colors flying,
  And now turn home again ashamed.
The ocean is our only refuge,
  The sandbank is our only goal,
The masts are swaying as with terror,
  And quivering does the vessel roll.
The mad wind frolics with the billows,
  Now smooths them low, now lashes high.
Now they are storming up like lions,
  And now like serpents sleek they lie;
And wave on wave is ever pressing,
  They hiss, they whisper, soft of tone.
Alack! was that the vessel splitting?
  Are sail and mast and rudder gone?
Here, screams of fright, there, silent weeping,
  The bravest feels his courage fail,
What stead our prudence or our wisdom?
  The soul itself can naught avail.

And each one to his God is crying,
    Soar up, my soul, to Him aspire,
Who wrought a miracle for Jordan,
    Extol Him, oh angelic choir!
Remember Him who stays the tempest,
    The stormy billows doth control,
Who quickeneth the lifeless body,
    And fills the empty frame with soul
Behold! once more appears a wonder,
    The angry waves erst raging wild,
Like quiet flocks of sheep reposing,
    So soft, so still, so gently mild
The sun descends, and high in heaven,
    The golden-circled moon doth stand.
Within the sea the stars are straying,
    Like wanderers in an unknown land
The lights celestial in the waters
    Are flaming clearly as above,
As though the very heavens descended
    To seal a covenant of love.
Perchance both sea and sky, twin oceans,
    From the same source of grace are sprung
'Twixt these my heart, a third sea, surges,
    With songs resounding, clearly sung.

II.

A watery waste the sinful world has grown,
With no dry spot whereon the eye can rest
No man, no beast, no bird to gaze upon,
Can all be dead, with silent sleep possessed?
Oh, how I long the hills and vales to see,
To find myself on barren steppes were bliss.
I peer about, but nothing greeteth me,
Naught save the ship, the clouds, the waves' abyss,
The crocodile which rushes from the deeps;
The flood foams gray; the whirling waters reel,
Now like its prey whereon at last it sweeps,
The ocean swallows up the vessel's keel.
The billows rage—exult, oh soul of mine,
Soon shalt thou enter the Lord's sacred shrine!

ISRAEL, THE DOVE.*

I

Thy undefiled dove,
Thy fondling, Thy love.
That once had, all blest,
In Thy bosom her nest—
Why dost Thou forsake her
Alone in the forest?
And standest aloof,
When her need is the sorest?
While everywhere
Threatens snare;
Strangers stand around her,
And strive night and day
To lead her astray,
While in silence she,
In the dead of night,
Looks up to Thee,
Her sole delight.
Dost Thou not hear,
Her voice sweet and clear:
Wilt aye thou forsake me?
"My darling, my One!
And I know that beside Thee,
Redeemer, there's none!"

II.

How long will Thy dove
Thus restlessly rove
In the desert so wild,
Mocked and reviled?
And the maid-servant's son
Came furiously on,
Dart after dart.
Pierced through my heart,
Horrid birds of prey
Lie soft in my nest,
While I, without rest,
Roam far, far away.
And still I am waiting
And contemplating;
And counting the days,
And counting the years.,
The miracles ceased
No prophet appears;
And wishing to learn

* Translated by Prof E Lowenthal.

About Thy return.
And asking my sages:
"Is the end drawing nigh?"
They sadly reply:
"That day and that hour
But to him are known.
And I know that beside Thee,
Redeemer, there's none!"

III.

And my wee, cooing dear ones,
The bright and the clear ones,
Were dragged in their slumbers
By infinite numbers
Of vultures so horrid
To cold climes and torrid,
Far, far away.
And those birds of prey
Try to render them faithless,
And make them give up
Thee, their sole Hope!
To turn their affection
From Thee, O Perfection!
Thou Friend of the Friendless!
Thou Beauty endless!
Ah, where art thou?
My Darling, My One !
My foes are near,
My Friend is gone.
Fainting in sorrow,
I'm here all alone.
And I know that beside Thee,
Redeemer, there's none!

IV.

Oh, hasten, my Love,
To Thy poor, timid dove!
They trample with their feet me,
They laugh when I mourn;
There's no friend to greet me,
I am all forlorn!
My foes in their passion,
And wild frantic ire,
Employ sword and fire,
And all kinds of tortures,
And know no compassion
They drive from land to land me:
There's none to befriend me.
The stars there on high
Hear me silently moan.
And I know that beside Thee,
Redeemer, there's none!

V.

Didst Thou reject me?
Dost love me no more?
Didst Thou forget all
Thy promises of yore?
Oh, rend Thy heavens !
Oh, come down again!
My enemies may see
That I, not in vain,
Have trusted in Thee.
As once upon Sinai,
Come down, my sole Dear
In Thy majesty appear!
Hurl down from his throne,
The maid-servant's son!
And strength impart
To my fainting heart,
Ere sadly I wander
To the land unknown.
For I know that beside Thee,
Redeemer, there's none!

Noble Ha-Levi, poet by the grace of God humbly we implore thy pardon for so feebly speaking of thee and thy glorious work! Would that we had the gift to speak of thee as thou deservest. Fill us thou sweet singer of Israel, with poetic instinct, and fill us, too, with thy religious zeal and fervor. Fill us with such a love for Israel and her cause, that we too might as thou didst toil for the of our people and our God. *

"Oh! city of the world, most chastely fair;
In the far west, behold I sigh for thee,
And in my yearning love I do bethink me
Of bygone ages ; of thy ruined fame,
Thy vanished splendor of a vanished day.
Oh! had I eagles' wings I'd fly to thee,
And with my falling tears make moist thine earth.
I long for thee ; though indeed thy kings
Have passed forever ; what though where once uprose
Sweet balsam trees, the serpent makes his nest ;
Oh· that I might embrace thy dust, the sod
Were sweet as honey to my fond desire."

* Translated by Mrs. Magnus

The above poetic translations are for the most part selected from "Songs of a Semite" by Miss Emma Lazarus.

CHAP. XIII.

IN PHILOSOPHY.

ALEXANDRIA, THE INTELLECTUAL METROPOLIS OF THE WORLD.—A
PRODIGIOUS STIMULUS GIVEN TO LEARNING.—THE SEPTUAGINT. —DE
VELOPMENT OF GRECIAN PHILOSOPHY INTO ARISTOTLIANISM.
THIS ENGRAFTED ON JEWISH THEOLOGY.—OPPOSITION
OF CHRISTIANITY TO ARISTOTLIANISM.—AVER-
ROES —MOSES MAIMONIDES.—OPPO-
SITION UNSUCCESSFUL

We must devote some little space and time to
a review of the place the Moors and the Jews
held in philosophy during their stay in Spain
from the eight to the fifteenth century. The purpose of this work makes this review necessary.
Not that we shall see any wonderful advance in
this department of learning, nor that we need
show the glaring contrast between the sophistical cobwebs of the cotemporaneous scholastics
and the rational researches of the Moorish and
Jewish philosophers, but that we may see what a
debt of gratitude modern philosophy owes the
Jew and Moor, for taking up the thread of phil-
osphical research where Greek intelligence had
been forced to leave it, and for carrying it forward sufficiently for modern philosophy to build

upon it, as a superstructure, the theories and
systems of to-day.

To fully understand their place in philosophy
it is necessary for us to retrace our steps in history some 2,000 years, and enter the city of
Alexandria. Here Alexander the Great had established his seat of government. It became the
intellectual metropolis of the world. Thither the
conqueror brought the wealth and learning of the
globe. Into that city the people streamed, or
were brought as prisoners, from the remotest
corners of the known world, from the Danube to
the Nile, and from the Nile to the Ganges. For
the first time in the world's history, there could
be found in one city, men who could speak learn-
edly of the Borean blasts of the countries beyond
the Black Sea, and of the simoons of the Oriental
deserts, of pyramids and obelisks and sphinxes
and hieroglyphics, of the Persian and Assyrian
and Babylonian wonders, of the Chaldean astronomers, of hanging gardens, aqueducts, hydraulic
machinery, tunnels under the river-bed, or of the
Assyrian method of printing, on plastic clay.
For the first time in the world's history seekers
after knowledge could listen, in the Serapion of
Alexandria, to learned discussions between Jewish monotheists and Persian dualists and Grecian
polytheists and Egyptian mysticists and. Indian
Brahmanists and Buddhists, and between the
Ionics and Pythagoreans, and Eleatics and the
Atomists and Anaxagoreans, and the Socratists,
and Platonists and Aristotelians and Stoics and
Epicureans and Neo-Platonists. No age or

city had ever furnished better opportunities for intellectual pursuits. No city could ever before this, point to kings more enthusiastic for the promotion of learning than were her Ptolemys, nor could all antiquity boast of a library equal to hers, or of a museum as justly celebrated for its botanical gardens and astronomical observatories and anatomical college and chemical labratory,

A prodigious stimulus was thus given to learning, and it has left its impress upon the world's civilization. Here Euclid wrote the theorems which are still studied by the college students of to day. Here Archimedes studied mathematics under Conon. Here Eratosthones made astronomy a science. Here Ptolemy wrote his "Syntaxes." Here Ctesibius and Hero invented the steam engine. Here true philosophy flourished, and for the first time, too, in the world's history. The people of the Orient had dabbled in speculative thought before this, but the results achieved showed that the Oriental mind is not adapted to abstract reasoning. The luxurious habits and voluptuous surroundings and tropical climate of the Orient tend more toward poetry, music and love and languor than toward psychical contemplations. The awe-awakening phenomena of nature, which confront the Oriental everywhere, naturally lead him to accept as *a priori* principles what the philosophers of the Occident make the subject of endless, and for the most part, incomprehensible and unsatisfactory systems of philosophy.

It is for this reason that the great religons

of the world sprang from Oriental soil, while the great philosophical systems took roots in Western lands. Yet, up to this period, not even the West, with all its labors, had sounded the depths of true philosophy. The entire pre-Socratic philosophy wasted its energies upon the futile effort to find some principle for the explanation of nature, which to the Hebrew mind had been solved thousands of years before in the opening verse of the Bible. One thought it to be *water;* another, *air;* and a third an original *chaotic matter.* The Pythagoreans declared that *number* is the essence of all things, and the Eleatics believed they were nearer the truth by negating all division in space and time. The Atomists endowed each atom with gravity and motion, and accounted thus for the origin of all physical existences and states. Socrates and Plato both came much nearer to the solution of the problem; the former postulated self-knowledge as the starting point of all philosophy, and the latter combined all preceding systems into one scheme, with an *infinitely wise and just and powerful spirit* as its guiding principle, but idealistically only, The additional realistic view of things had not yet been reached, and could not be reached, for that depends upon universal and exact and scientific knowledge, which prior to the great age of Alexandrian learning, to which all ages and climes and nations contributed their experiences and observation and knowledge, had never yet existed. Aristotle, the teacher of Alexander, and the friend of Ptolemy, thus found through

Alexandrian influence, opportunities for philosophical reasoning, which necessarily gave his
system an almost inestimable advantage over his
predecessors.   From the study of particulars he
rose to a knowledge of universals, advancing to
them by induction.   This inductive method was
grounded upon facts of his own experience and observation, as well as those of others, whom the intellectual metropolis had sent into Greece.   He
oecame the first and best absolute empiricist. His
system acquired an encyclopedic character.   He
became the father of logic, natural history, empirical pyschology and the science ot rights.
Aristotelian philosophy became the intellectual
corner stone on which the Museum rested, and is
tu-day, through Jewish and Moorish influence, as
we shall presently see, the corner stone of modern philosophy.

The Jewish community of Alexandria was very
large.   When Alexander founded this city and
gave it his name, he wished to secure for it permanent success, and so he brought them thither
by the thousands.   Ptolemy brought 100,-
000 more, after his siege of Jerusalem, and Phil-
adelphus, his successor, redeemed from slavery
198,000 Jews, "paying their Egyptian owners a
just money equivalent for each."   Alexander's
expectations were realized; the city of his name
led the world in commerce and intellect.   With
an enthusiasm almost bordering on passion the
Hebrews devoted themselves to philosophy, especially to Aristotelian philosophy.   They in-
grafted it upon their own theology and philo-

sophic speculations, some going even so far as
to believe that Aristotle must have been a Jew
himself.

Henceforth Aristotelian philosophy is Jewish
philosophy. The occasional acceptance of the
Neo-Platonic mysticism, theosophy and theurgy,
was unable to obliterate it.

During seven centuries learning flourished in
the city of Alexandria, zealously fostered by native Egyptian, Greek and Jew. A new power
arose—Christianity. At once it recognized in
Aristotelian philosophy an inimical foe, and began its work of suppressing rational research and
free thought. The rest we need not relate. We
know what happens when Christianity institutes
inquisitors of faith instead of inquirers of learning. We know what happens when Christianity
uses power instead of argument. That day,
when the beautiful and young Hypatia, perhaps,
the most accomplished woman that has ever
lived, the popular lecturer of Platonic and Aristotelian philosophy at the Museum, where her
lecture room was crowded daily, with the wealth
and intellect of Alexandria; that day, when this
most noble of women was assaulted by Bishop
Cyril's fanatical and bloodthristy monks, when
she was dragged by the followers of the "religion
of love," from her chariot, stripped naked in the
street, pulled into the church, where she was cut
to pieces—where her flesh was scraped from the
bones with a shell and the remnants cast into fire;
that day marked the extinction of Alexandrian
learning—it marked the extinction of Athenian

learning. Science, so successful, died the death
of strangulation, and the expounders of Aristotelian philosophy were silenced, and their literature
condemned to the pyre.

But Aristotelian philosophy was not yet dead.
The Jews still lived, and with them the works of
Aristotle. They had succeeded in concealing
translations and original copies of his works from
the fanatical champions of ignorance. They had
absorbed it into their system of thought. They
had used it in their commentaries upon their
Scriptures. They had saturated their very
prayers with it. They had sought to reconcile
Jewish theology with refined heathen philosophy.
Whither they wandered, it wandered, and where
they were permitted to study there also was Aristotelian philosophy studied. What they had long
wished was granted them at last. They became
the restorers of philosophy in Europe. Moorish
and Spanish prosperity afforded them the opportunities for an uninterrupted study and development of the Aristotelian philosophy. Soon the
Moor shared their enthusiasm. The caliphs sent
special messengers to secure whatever of Aristotelian philosophy had escaped the mob of "St.
Cyril." *

Many were they, both Jews and Moors, who
devoted themselves to this philosophy, and vast
the systems they unfolded. The wonderful ad-

---

* Cyril has the title of "St." now; when first we met him, instigating
his monks to ki'l the learned Hypatia, he was only Bishop Cyril. That
noble and humane act together with his commendable zeal for throttling
science and rational research has won for him the honored title of "St."

vance they had made in the sciences, and in the other branches of learning, enabled them to enlarge upon the teachings of Aristotle. New facts and new experiences and new observatious led them to new and advanced inductions. However great the tempations be to enter into some analysis of their philosophical system, we must not yield to them; that is not the object of this review. Our design is to show what influence Moorish and Jewish learning exercised upon European civilization. We have seen its impress upon the sciences and literatures of Europe, and its impress is visible still on modern philosophy. * From all parts of the world persons having a taste for philosophy found their way to the Moorish and Jewish sages of Spain. Gerbet himself, later Pope Sylvester II., had repaired to Cordova and Seville to hear Moorish and Jewish philosophers expound the mysteries of wisdom and philosophy, and so illustrious an example soon became the raging fashion among European scholars. As if desirous of dividing the honors equally, both the Moors and the Jews sent at the same time, a representative champion into the philosophical arena who, by their united labors, not only demolished scholasticism but also laid the permanent foundation of modern philosophy. The representative philosopher of the Moors was the great Averroes

---

* As a careful study of Eisler's "Vorlesungen Ueber Juedische Philosophie des Mittelalters," and Renan's "Averroes et Averoisme," and Joel's "Verhaltniss Albert des Grossen zu Moses Maimonides," and "Spinoza's Theolgo-Politischer Traktat auf Seine Quellen's Geprueft," and Haarbruecker's translation of Schahrastani's "Religions Partheien Philosophen-Schulen," will readily prove.

(Ibn Roshd, 1149-1198) whose name still occupies an honored place upon the pages of history of philosophy, and whose system, bearing his name—Averroism—is still recognized among the philosophical systems of the world. The representative Jewish philosopher was the great Moses Maimonides, (1135-1204) the greatest Jewish philosopher the Jews have ever produced, and one of the greatest the world has seen to this day, whose philosophical system, unfolded in his "More Nebuchim," ("Guide for the Perplexed") still remains truly, grandly immortal.

For several centuries the Moorish and Jewish philosphy was the delight of such men in whom Spanish learning kindled a desire for deeper research and loftier thought than Europe had bitherto offered. Even many of the schoolmen shared this enthusiasm. But this very enthusiasm was the deathblow to scholasticism. Once imbued with Moorish and Jewish empirical philosophy and inductive reasoning, the rational mind could no longer pursue the sophistic teachings which the church held up as the divine wisdom. That philosophy shook the old faith to its very root, produced new predispositions and prepared the way for the coming change. It weaned men from simply believing the church's "say-so" and taught them to think, and when men began to think scholasticism ceased, and the Reformation began, and with it modern thought. No longer would the rational mind believe that legends and miracles can decide such questions as are the starting point of philosophic thought. No

longer would they endure the preposterous teaching—the product of ignorance and audacity—
that the faith of the church is absolute truth; that
faith is greater than knowledge; that a thing may
be theologically true even though it be philosoph-
ically false. No longer would they disgrace
themselves with continuing to waste time and
parchment with discussions and treatises such as
these, to which the schoolmen of several centuries devoted hundreds of volumes: "How many
choirs of angels are there in heaven, how do
they sit and upon what instrument do they play?
"To what temperature does the heat rise in hell?"
"Wherein lies the difference between 'consub-
stantiatio and transubstantiato'?" "What kind of
feathers had the angel Gabriel in his wings?
What kind of a swallow it was that caused Tobias
blindness? Whether Pilate washed his hands
with soap before he condemned Jesus? Whether
it was an adagio or allegro which David played
before Saul? What sort of salve it was which
Mary brought to the Lord? Whether the coat
for which the soldiers cast lots constituted the
entire raiment of the Redeemer? Whether the
valley of Jehosophat is large enough for the
world's judgment day?" and so on *ad nauseam.*
A schism arose. The indignation of St. Thomas
Aquinas, the leader of the Dominicans, knew no
bounds when he beheld Christians drinking in, in
full draughts, Moorish and Jewish philosophy.
The Franciscans opposed him and every effort of
his to suppress their writings. The conflict lasted
till 1512, when the Lateran council condemned

"the abettors of these detestable doctrines to be
held as heretics and infidels," and the Dominicans,
armed with the weapons of the Inquisition, were
not slow to silence Averoism in Europe.

But though silenced it lived in Jewish philosophy, and that, as little as its Talmud and Bible
no power on earth has ever been strong enough
to silence. Though silenced, with the aid of the
Jews it flashed forth to all parts of Europe, where
it found its way as readily into the "Opus Majus"
of Roger Bacon as into the curriculum of studies of the University of Padua. Though silenced,
it permeated the Renaissance. Though silenced,
it formed the groundwork of Spinoza's system.
Though silenced, with the aid of the Jewish philosophers, who laughed the Inquisition to scorn,
it was studied everywhere, and everywhere it
assumed those gigantic proportions destined to
illumine the intellect of Europe. Though silenced, with the aid of the Jewish philosophy it,
ushered in modern philosophy and the civilization
of to-day.

CHAP. XIV.

IN THE INDUSTRIES.

INTELLECTUAL GREATNESS OF MOORS AND JEWS INDUCED BY THEIR MA
TERIAL PROSPERITY—REMARKABLE DEVELOPMENT OF AGRICULTURE
—NEW DISCOVERIES IN EVERY INDUSTRY—MINING A SPECIALTY
THE MAGNET. MARINER'S COMPASS MECHANICAL APPARATUS.
SPREAD OF COMMERCE LEADS TO GENERAL AWAKENING
OF EUROPE THAT ENDS MIDDLE AGES.

Hark! Again the doleful knell is tolling. With greater speed and in larger numbers the people are hurrying to the public square, The procession of priests, chanting hymns of victory and imprecatory prayers, is starting towards the auto-da-fe. The victims supplicate for death more piteously than before. Hark! Again, and with greater alarm, the agonized voice of civilization calls unto us: Haste ye, the furnaces are heated! The pyres are prepared! The massive gates of the gloomy inquisition dungeons are open. The instruments of torture are ready for the cruel work of death. Haste ye, the moments are few, gather whatever knowledge there still remains to be collected concerning the wondrous achievements of the Jew and Moor, as speedily as you can; tarry, and flame and sword and rack and expulsion will hurl all knowledge of it into oblivion forever!

Let us heed the warning and briefly state what
yet remains to be told. You have 'ere this sur-
mised what we are about to prove, the imperisha-
ble monuments which the Moors and Jews have
erected to their name and fame in the arts and
sciences, in literature and philosophy bear witness,
not only to their great intellectual wealth, but also to vast material possessions. Wherever learning is zealously fostered there wealth exists, and
where wealth abounds, there agriculture and
commerce and industry must have had prior existence.

Thus it was in Moorish Spain. Never before,
nor ever since, did Spain enjoy a prosperity equal
to that which blessed her lands, when Moorish
and Jewish skill and diligence and enterprise made
her, in glaring contrast with the rest of Europe,
the granary and the industrial and the commercial
center of the world. We have not yet forgotten how,
when in the introductory chapters of this volume,
we thought ourselves back some eight or ten centuries in the world's history, and hastened across
the wild Atlantic to learn of the condition of Europe and her people, how spell-bound we stood,
as we suddenly beheld wonders and beauties
in Spain, scarcely equalled to-day in all Europe.
And when we reflected upon the present condition
of Spain, among the poorest of all European
countries, its people proverbially indolent and
ignorant, we had to assure ourselves, again and
again, that it was Spain, indeed, which suddenly
disclosed to us these unexpected, and still un-
equalled, proofs of industry and learning and

cultured taste. Nor have we yet forgotten, when gliding upon the majestic Guadalquivir along fertile valleys, and luxuriant fields and graceful groves, and fragrant parks, and glittering palaces, and busy factories, and restless mines, we passed out of Spain, and visited the other countries of Europe how dreary and wretched and appalling the scenes were which met our gaze everywhere. Scarcely a city anywhere. Nothing that could, even with the broadest stretch of leniency, be designated as agriculture. Everywhere pathless deserts and howling wastes, and death-exhaling swamps. Wretched, windowless and chimneyless and floorless hovels sheltered man and beast under the same roof. Everywhere men with squalid beards, and women with hair unkempt and matted with filth, and both clothed in garments of untanned skin, that were kept on the body till they dropped in pieces of themselves, a loathsome mass of vermin, stench and rags. Everywhere beans and vetches and roots and bark of trees and horseflesh furnished largely the means of supporting life. Nowhere even a trace or semblance of industry. Everywhere the word commerce an unintilligible term. Such was the condition of the rest of Europe when Spain was basking in the sunshine of a most wonderful state of prosperity under the skill and enterprise of the Jew and the Moor.

From the very first both directed their attention to agriculture. The fertile valleys and the luxuriant fields, and the vine-clad hills, and the fruitful orchards, and the flowry meads and the sweet-scented pasture lands of Palestine bear eloquent testimony to Jewish skill in agriculture. The advice which the prophet Jeremiah had sent to the Jewish captives of Babylon : "Build ye houses, and dwell in them, and plant gardens and eat the fruits of them, ... and increase in your captivity and not diminish. Seek the welfare of the city whither you are carried as captives, and pray unto the Lord for it ; for in the welfare thereof shall ye prosper and have peace."* This excellent advice the Jews applied to themselves, and faithfully followed, wherever they lived in exile, and wherever they were suffered to dwell in peace and promote the country's welfare. The Arab-Moors were no less devoted to this noble pursuit. When their warfare was over they beat their swords into plowshares, and their spears into pruning knives. Their motto was : "He who planteth and soweth, and maketh the earth bring forth fruit for man and beast, hath done alms that shall be reckoned to him in heaven." These two races devoted themselves to the cultivation of Spain with their hereditary love for the occupation, and with the skillful application of the experience, which they had gathered in other lands where they had dwelled or where they had established their power. By them agriculture in Spain was carried to a height, which until the invention of machinery was not surpassed in Europe. As early as the tenth century the revenue of agriculture of Moorish Spain alone amounted to nearly $6,000,000, more than the entire revenue of all the rest of Europe at that time. The ruins of their noble works for the irrigation of the soil, their

---

* Jeremiah xxix : 5-8

great treaties on irrigation and crops, and im-
proved breeds of cattle, on grafting and gardening,
and their code of laws regulating agriculture, which
still exist, still attest their skill and industry and
put to shame the ignorance and indolence of their
Spanish successors. Many plants were introduced
in Europe, and successfully cultivated by them,
which, after the expulsion of the Jews and Moors,
and the discovery of America, Spain lost and
neglected, such as rice and sugar cane (*soukhar*,
as they called it, saffron and mulberry trees, ginger,
myrrh, bananas and dates. The Spanish names
of many plants show their origin, and some have
traveled even to us, such as the apricot, from
"*albaric aque*," the artichoke from "*alca chofa*,"
coton from "*al godon*." * They gave Xeres and
Malaga their celebrated wine, which has maintained
its reputation to this day.

The mining industries, too, were zealously
fostered by them.   Spain was and is a widely
metalliferous country.   Her hidden treasures were
known already to the Phœnieians, Carthagenians
and Romans, and were mined by them with great
profit.   The gold and silver of Solomon's temple
come through Hiram of Tyre from Tarshish, which
was Southern Spain.   But the dark ages had set
in and with them Europe's universal sloth.   When
the Moors entered Spain the ancient mines had
been, for the most part, abandoned.   They re-
vived this industry, and with a zeal which may best
be told by the existence to-day of 5,000 Moorish
shafts—distinguished from the former by being

---

* "Christians and Moors of Spain," by C. M. Yonge, chapter x.

square instead of round—in one district (Jaen) alone gold was found in large quantities, and it was one of their leading articles for manufacture and export. They gave us the Arabic word *"carat,"* which we still use in speaking of the quality of gold. They opened the inexhaustible vein of mercury which they worked with great profit and with such skill, that it still forms the largest deposit in the world, yielding still one-half of the quicksilver now in use, and being a government monopoly, this one remnant of Moorish and Jewish skill and industry, alone, still produces an annual revenue of $1,250,000. In addition to these, lead, copper, iron, alum, red and yellow ochre were mined in great quantity. Precious stones also were in great abundance—the beryl, ruby, golden marcasite, agates. garnets. Pearls were found on the coast near Barcelona. Building stones, marbles, and jaspers of all colors, were uninterruptedly quarried in the mountains.

The manufacturing industries kept pace in their success with that of mining and agriculture. With the Jews a knowledge of silk culture came into Europe, and with the assistance of Moorish skill it became one of the leading industries and one of the most profitable exports. All Europe, and the greater portions of Asia and Africa, looked to the Jews and Moors of Spain for their fine fabrics of silk and cotton and woolen, for all the wonders of the loom and the skilful and delicate patterns of filigree work in gold and silver. The carpet manufacture of the Moslems reached the excellence which it has maintained to our own day.

They made glass out of a silicious clay and used it for fashioning vessels, and also in glazing those beautiful tiles—for which Valencia is still famous—called *azulejos*, which they employed in embelishing floors and wainscoting. The best leather was made by the Jews and Arab-Moors in Cordova, and hence Spanish leather is still called *Cordovan*, which has given to English shoemakers their name of "Cordwainers" The still celebrated "Morocco" leather—the secret of its manufacture having been carried to Morocco, after their expulsion from Spain, —speaks to this day of Moorish and Jewish skill in this branch of industry. The "Toledo Blade," famous in the past and famous still, the invention of, and the plentiful and lucurative manufacture of cotton and linen paper, that blessed boon to civilization, which alone made the printing press possible and beneficial, the introduction of gunpowder and artillery, of the magnet and the mariner's compass, of mechanical and scientific apparatus and instruments, these and many more still speak in eloquent terms of Moorish and Jewish industry in Spain, and, more eloquently still, they tell the tale of Spanish ingratitude. *

---

*For details see Copee's "Conquest of Spain, " volume II chapter VIII and Prescott's "Ferdinand and Isabella," volume I, chapter VIII.

The Jews were the most skillful physicians, the ablest financiers, and among the most profound philosophers; while they were only second to the Moors in the cultivation of natural science. They were also the chief interpreters to western Europe of Arabian learning. But their most important service, and that with which we are now most especially concerned, was in sustaining commercial activity. For centuries they were its only representatives. By travelling from land to land till they became intimately acquainted both with the wants and the productions of each, by practising money-lending on a large scale and with consumate skill, by keeping up a constant and secret correspondence and organising a system of exchange that was then unparalled in Europe, the Jews succeeded in mak-

This diligence and success in agriculture and in the industries made commerce necessarily very active and lucrative. The ports swarmed with vessels of traffic. The Jews and Moors of Spain maintained a merchant marine of thousands of ships. They had their factories and warehouses and consuls in all centers of industry. Their exports were very large.

The Jews, who had been compelled to wander the wide world over had acquired a most perfect geographical knowledge, which was serviceable to them now. It was through them that the existence of the Cape of Good Hope was made known in Europe. It was through Averroes that the attention of Columbus was drawn to his subject of finding a short route to the Indies. Their commerce opened the tide of discovery by navigation. Moorish and Jewish industry sought foreign mar-

ing themselves absolutely indispensible to the Christian community, and and in accumulating immense wealth and acquiring immense influence in the midst of their sufferings. When the Italian republics rose to power, they soon became the centres to which the Jews flocked; and under the merchant goverments of Leghorn, Venice, Pisa, and Genoa, a degree of toleration was accorded that was indeed far from perfect, but was at last immeasureably greater than elsewhere, (From Lecky's "Rationalism in Europe," part II, Chapter VI.)

From the port of Barcelona the Spanish khalifs had carried on an enormous commerce, and they with their coadjutors—Jewish merchants —had adopted or originated many commercial inventions, which, with matters of pure science, they had transmitted to the trading communities of Europe, The art of book-keeping by double entry was thus brought into Upper Italy. The different kinds of insurance were adopted, though strenuously resisted by the clergy- They opposed fire and marine insurance, on the ground that it was a tempting of Providence. Life insurance was regarded as an act of interference with the consequences of God's will. Houses for lending money on interest, that is, banking establishments, were bitterly denounced, and especially was indignation excited against the taking of high rates of interests, which was stigmatized as usury—a feeling existing in some backward communities up to the present day. Bills of exchange in the present form were adopted, the office of the public no-

kets and found them, too, from the Azores to the
interior of China, from the Baltic to the coast of
Mozambique, and eventually from the kingdom of
Granda to the new world. Granada, especially in
the words of the historian, became the common
city of all nations. The reputation of its citizens
for trustworthiness was such that their bare word
was more relied on than a written contract is now
among us, to which a Catholic bishop adds :
"Moorish integrity is all that is necessary to make
a good Christian."*

*Conde's "History of the Arabs of Spain," volumn III, chapter XXVI.

tary established, and protests for dishonored obligations resorted to. In
deed, it may be said, with but little exaggeration, that the commercial
machinery now used was thus introduced. (Draper's "Conflict between Religion and Science," Chapter XI, pg. 317—318)

"The isolation in which the Jews were forced to live, and the prohibitions
long continued, against acquiring real estate, directed their speculations
toward commerce and manufactures, in which they soon obtained incontestable superiority. . . . Nothing is more curious to study than the commercial condition of that nation which had no territory of its own, nor
ports, nor armies, and which, constantly tacking about on an agitated
sea, with contrary winds, at last arrived in port with rich cargoes and
immense wealth. The Jews traded because it was rarely permitted them to
employ themselves in any other way with security. While the multiplicity
of toll-houses and the tyranny of the feudal lords rendered all trade impossible except that of the petty tradesmen of the market-towns and
cities, the Jews, more bold, more mobile, were dreaming of vaster operations. and were working silently to bind together continents, to bring
together kingdoms. They avoided the highways and the castles, carefully concealing their real opulence and their secret transactions under
the appearances of poverty. They went great distances for rare products
of the remote countries, and brought them within reach of well-to-do
consumers. By wandering about and traveling from country to country
they had acquired an exact acquaintance with the needs of all places ;
they knew where to buy and where to sell. Some samples and a note-
book sufficed them for their most important operations. They corre-
sponded with each other on the strength of engagements which their
interest obliged them to respect, in view of the enemies of every sort by
whom they were surrounded. Commerce has lost the trace of the in-
genous inventions which were the result of their efforts ; but it is to their
influence that it owes the rapid progress of which histore shows us the

The position of the Moors and Jews of Spain in
the industries may, therefore, be briefly summar-
ized thus, a prosperous state of commerce arose
never known before, and in the southern part of
Europe never equalled since.   Farther and farther
this commerce pushed its interests, and more and
more busy became the industries at home. and greater and greater grew their opulence. Gradually the
rest of Europe awakened from its lethargy. Moorish and Jewish toil infused life and ambition into
its people.   Italy, Portugal, France and England

---

briliant phenomenon in the midst of the horrois of feudal darkness
Inslensibly, the Jews were absorbing all the money, since this was the
kind of property which they could acquire and keep safely. . . . For
more than five hundred years, it is in the history of that nation that we
must study the progress of commerce and the more or less venturesome
attempts through which it has risen to the rank of political power. .
The Jews were the depositaries of the finest cloths known, and they traded
in them at immense profits : they extended the use and at the same time
the demand for them into castles and into abbeys.   They also engrossed
the trade in jewelry and in gold and silver bullion   Feudalism disturbed
these lucrative occupations less than one might suppose : the lords put
upon them stiict conditions, but they had the good sense to treat them
with respect.   Besides in the midst of the general terror which continually
hovered around all highways and all travelers, the Jews, armed with
safe-conducts, traveled all over Europe without inquietude, and in the
tenth and eleventh centuries disposed like sovereigns of all the commerce of France.   At that period, they had already greatly simplified
commercial proceedings, and their correspondence would have done honor
to the most able merchants of our great cities

The appearance of the tradesmen of Lombardy, Tuscany, and other
parts of Italy completed the work of the Jews and gave an energetic im-
pulse to the commerce of the middle ages.   The latter, from that time,
traded in everytning, and put in circulation real and peisonal property,
such as horses, lands and houses.   The historian Rigord goes so far as
to say that the Jews were, at that time, real proprietors of half the kingdom. . . .   It is also claimed that it was at this time that the first Bills
of Exchange appeared, the invention of which some trace to about the
seventh century, and others, only to the middle of the twelfth.   It is a
point which has not yet been cleared up, and which is not of so much
consequence as some have supposed.   The date of such a discovery,
even if it could be authentically fixed, would be of interest simply as a
matter of curiosity; but it appears destined to remain forever in doubt.
It is thought, and with reason, that the invention is rather due to the

began to compete.   New markets became necessary. New discoveries followed, and with the
general activity and prosperity which ensued, and
the learning which it fostered, it dispelled the
mists of ignorance, the middle ages disappeared and

Italian traders than to the Jewish brokers of this time, the latter not hav
ing had occasion as soon as the others to devote themselves to trade between different places, which probab'y suggested the idea.   The very
name of Letter of Exchange, which was primitively Italian. seems to indicate their true authorship; and the first city wheie they were used, Lyons,
then the entrepot of Italy, is a further indication.   It is probable that the
Lombards and the Jews had an equal part in inverting them, and divined, from the beginning, the important consequences from their use. * *
These ingenious contrivers later entered into a strife, and the histcry of
the Italian republics of the middle ages is full of the debates which arose
between them on the subject of privileges which some wished to exercise to
the exclusion of others   We see the Jews become intendants, stewards,
procurators, bankers, and even agents in marriages, according as they are
more or less forcibly driven from all the regular commercial positions by
the bulls of the Popes or by the jealousy of competitors.   Everything
thus contributed to narrow them down to a vicious circle, from which
they can only escape by usury and money negotiations   When envy
has forced them to abandon a city, the interest of the inhabitants calls
them back; their capital has become so necessary to their industrial cities
that the orders of the authorities are disregarded to prevent the Jews
carrying it elsewhere.   Moreover, soon houses for loaning money are
started even in the villages; and the Jews of Tuscany direct from a cen-
tral point a multitude of branch-houses of their establishments at Flor-
ence and Pisa,   Their opulence and their magnificence surpassed imagination, and aroused against them fanatical adversaries.   We know the
history of that famous Bernardin de Feltre, who carried his enthusiasm
so far as to preach a crusade against them, and who on every occasion
showed himself their most implacable enemy   He pursued them everywhere as usurers thirsting for the blood of the people, and, to ruin their
establishments, he conceived the idea of opposing them by the formation
of those houses of loaning on pledges, which are called *monts-de-piete*.
At the beginning, everything was fiee in them, and the sums lent were
without interest.   Morever, their success was prodigious, and most of the
cities of Italy had their *monts-de-piete*, which were one day to surpass in
usurious exactions the boldest operations of the Jews. . . .   However
these *monts-de-piete* could not fill the place of the establishments of the
Jews, and this circumstance proves with what shrewdness the latter   had
truly divined the wants of the money circulation. Although the *monts-de-
piete* loaned money almost without interest, the formalities which it was
necessary to undergo in oider to have a right to their help, the inevita-
ble delays in their administration, the necessity of prcving the legitimate
possession of the articles pledged, and above all, the obligation on the

modern history made its appearance upon the world's stage. So glorious was the result of Moorish and Jewish industry. How Europe rewarded them in return for all their lnbors, let the followiug chapters speak.

part of depositors to make known their names, soon kept away borrowers, who could obtain funds at any time, in secret and without formalities, from the Jewish bankers. Rich and poor, lords and villeins, hastened to them, and their credit was so great at Leghorn, in the times of the Medicis, that the saying became proverbial: *"It is better to beat the Grand-duke than a Jew."* Pope Sixtus-Fifth had opened again to them all the sources of wealth which his predecessors had closed; their goods were even exempt from every toll, the *sacra monte della pieta* ceased to compete with them, when the Christians in charge had surpassed the abuses of their rivals. After ten years of its existence, the *monts-de-piete* had become what they are to-day, open pits under the steps of misfortune rather than asylums to escape it. . . . Everything then seems to warrant the belief that the Jews exerccise a notable influence on the course of political economy in Europe, by keeping in charge, in the midst of feudal anarchy, the commercial traditions destined to become perfected and refined in the atmosphere of the fifteenth century. It is to the persecutions of which they were victims that we are indebted for the first attempts at credit and the system of circulation They alone, perhaps, by concentrating on trade in gold and silver an attention whicn the prejudices of their contemporaries prevented them from giving to anything else, prepared the way for the great monetary revolution which the discovery of the mines in America and the establishment of European banks were to accomplish in the world. Thus the luminous trace of the future shines and is preserved, in the midst even of the darkest events.

—"History of Political Economy in Europe," by Jerome Adolphe Blanqui Chap, XV.

CHAP. XV.

THE INQUISITION.

JEWISH AND MOORISH INTELLECTUAL ADVANCE FOLLOWED BY PHYSICAL
DECLINE—THIS DECLINE THE CAUSE OF THEIR DOWNFALL—THE
SPANIARD AGAIN RULER OVER SPAIN—THE INQUISITION ESTAB-
LISHED—TO ESCAPE IT JEWS BECOME "NEW CHRISTIANS"
—CHRISTIANITY NO HELP TO THE JEWS—THOMAS DE
TORQUEMADA—THE TORTURES OF THE INQUISITION
A PUBLIC BURNING.

Physical decline follows mental advance. The nation that is devoted to learning is not the nation that worships a military life, or the pursuits of warfare. When the Mohammedans started on the enterprise of acquiring vast territorial posses- sions, there were few nations, if any, that could stand before them; when they were bent upon making intellectual acquisitions, there was no milit- ary body in Europe so poor that could not over- throw them. The military and patriotic virtues of the Arab-Moors had slowly passed away. Their original simplicity had been replaced by the ex- travagance of Oriental luxury, and their early de- votedness to the Moslem faith had suffered much from their philosophical and scientific researches. *

* Coppee's "Conquest of Spain," Vol. 1, Chap. v, pp. 441-2.

Internecine wars among themselves hastened their decline. Faster and faster their once invincible power slipped from their hands. Faster and faster advanced the Spanish hosts. Arab-Moor and Spanish Christian met at last on the plains of "Las Navas," (1213) and the great defeat which the Moslem army sustained here marked the beginning of the fatal hour. City after city, province after province, they were forced to yield. At last, all was lost, save the city of Granada, which stood alone to represent the Mohammedan dominion in the peninsula. And, for a time, it seemed as if that noble city, the city of the Alhambra, the pride of the Moors, would not only represent the Mohammedan dominion, and stay the victorious advance of the Spanish hosts, but also regain all that had been lost.

But the ancient valor was aroused too late. Ferdinand, of Aragon, had married Isabella, of Castile. Two of the most powerful crowns and armies were united, and unitedly they marched against the city of Granada.

Granada surrendered. On the second day of January, 1492, the last and ill-fated king of the Moors, Boabdil (Abu Abdillah,) met Ferdinand and his party at the entrance of the Alhambra, and presenting the keys of the city, thus he spoke in a loud voice and in sad accents:

"We are thine, O powerful and exalted king ; these are the keys of this paradise. We deliver into thy hands this city and kingdom, for such is the will of Allah: and we trust thou wilt use thy triumph with generosity and clemency."

"We trust thy wilt use thy triumph with generosity and clemency." Did Boabdil have a foreboding of the infamous use the victor would make of his triumph? Did he really expect that his appeal for generosity and clemency would be favorably answered? If so, poor Boabdil, vain is thy hope, foolish thy trust. That hour in which the Christian *cross* replaced the Mohammedan *crescent* on the turret of the Alhambra, that hour when Christianity ruled again, and alone, in the peninsula, marked a climax in the history of cruelties and human sufferings. That hour, though the brightest in the reign of Ferdinand and Isabella, was most fatal for Spain, most pitiful to Europe, most unfortunate for civilization, and most calamitous for the Jews.

During all these unfortunate years of struggle for supremacy between the Mohammedan and Christian hosts the Jews were not forgotten. Sad as was the lot of the Moors, that of the Jews were inexpressibly more miserable. The Moors were conquered by soldiers, the Jews by monks. The Moors fought against the military of Spain, the Jews were inhumanly slaughtered by the "militia of Christ." The Moors suffered the pangs of war, and the Jews writhed in agony under the tortures of the Inquisition.

Inquisition! Who can utter the execrable word without a shudder! Who can think of this blood-thirsty institution without heaving a sigh of relief that it lasts no longer! What Jew can think of it with dry eyes, without lifting his heart to God in thanksgiving that this blood-reeking tribunal is no more!

Inquisition! Who knows its meaning better than the Jews? What people brought greater sacrifice to its bloody altars than they? Who has described it better than the Jew, *Samuel Usque*, the Jewish poet, whose lyre was silenced, and whose life was tortured out of his body by that very institution which he so eloquently and truthfully describes? "From Rome," he says, "a beast most monstrous, most ferocious, and most foul has come into our midst. Its very appearance strikes terror into every soul. When it raises its piercing, hissing, seething voice all Europe trembles. Its body is made of a composition of the hardest of steel and the deadliest of poison. In strength, in capacity for murder, in size and in speed it excels the fiercest of lions, the most poisonous of serpents, the tallest of elephants, and the speediest of eagles. Its very voice will kill quicker than the bite of the basilisk. Fire issues from its eyes, its jaws breathe forth flames. It lives from human bodies only. Wherever it comes, and though the sunshine in its noontide brightness, the densest darkness will at once set in. In its presence every blade of grass, every flower and blossom and tree, all wither and perish. Wherever it passes its pestiferous stench changes fertile valleys and luxurious fields and laughing meadows into unproductive deserts and howling wastes. Its name is *The Inquisition.*"

It was born in the early part of the thirteenth century. Fanaticism was its mother; its father was St. Dominic, who also was the father of the Dominican Order, and so the Inquisition and the Dominican friars were natural brothers, and "par nobile fratrum," a noble pair of brothers they were. Pope Innocent III. stood godfather to it. I fully sympathize with all past and present humanitarians in their efforts to wean men from the pernicious belief in the existence of Hell, but I can not accept their claims that Hell never existed. Hell did exist, not 10,000 leagues beneath the earth, but on its very face. Hell existed wherever the Inquisition lived. And Devils there were, too, and their names were "Dominican Monks." This ferocious beast-child came into this world with a mission: to detect, punish and suppress Heresy Free Thought, and every Religious belief save that of the Church of St. Peter. Under Dominican nursing and training, it grew and prospered, and rapidly acquired a relentless exercise of its mission. Its heart was killed, its conscience stifled. It was never taught the meaning of the words pity and mercy.

Scarcely was it full grown when it initiated its bloody career of 600 years of accursed life by a most cruel reign of terror in the southern provinces of France, where the presence and strength of the heretical *Albigenses* and where the Moorish and Jewish civilization from across the Pyrenes had made themselves felt. The reign of terror ceased with the extermination of almost the entire population.

At last it found its way into Spain, and in that country it entered upon a career so infamous that

its deeds of ferocity, recorded upon the annals
of History in letters of blood and fire, are not
eclipsed by the combined cruelties of all mankind.
Here lived and prospered thousands and thousands
of Jews. When a holy war is waged against the
infidel Moors shall the infidel Jews escape un-
scathed? When the Blessed Virgin crowns their
zeal to their faith by giving them victory after
victory over the Moors, will she not be wroth if the
Jews escape? When the Moors are put to the
edge of the sword, shall the Jews not be committed
to the flames?

The cruelties of the Inquisition were not the
first which were visited upon the Jews. Their
second series of suffering in Spain began on the
day when the Christian forces defeated the Moor
ish army upon the battle-field. The tolerance the
Moor could afford to offer to the Jew, the Re
ligion of Christ could not. In Aragon and Castile
it was not a rare sight to see the fanatical populace,
stimulated by the no less fanatical clergy, to
make a fierce assault upon this unfortunate people
—guilty of no other crime than that of promoting
the prosperity of Spain and of adhering to their in-
herited belief,—breaking into their houses, violating their most private sanctuaries, and consigning
them by the thousands to indiscriminate massacre,
without regard to sex or age. Hatred of the Jews
was for many centuries a faithful index of the
piety of the Christians. Cruel laws were enacted
against them. They were prohibited from ming-
ling freely with the Christians, from following the
trades and professions for which they were best

suited by virtue of their high intelligence and thrift. Their residence was restricted within certain prescribed limits of the cities which they inhabited. They were held up to continuous public scorn, by being compelled to wear a peculiar dress, on which was sewed their badge of shame. Even in their executions they were branded, for a long time they were hanged between two dogs, and with the head downwards.

A choice was given them to escape these sufferings and degradations by entering "the religion of love unto all men." Thousands upon thousands of Jews availed themselves of this only alternative, and became feigned converts, or "new Christians," as they were called. They amply regretted the change later, but at present it seemed to them an almost justifiable step. The preceding chapters have acquainted us with the character of the Spanish Jews, with their high intellectual attain ments, with their lofty demeanor, with their high social and political and industrial and commercial standing. Think of them now asked to sacrifice all these advantages, because the iron-handed and iron-hearted brute force of the priests so wanted it. Feel as they must have felt, when they were asked to exchange their mansions of elegance and refinement for the wretched hovels of the Ghetto; to lay aside their garments of silk, and their ornaments of grace and beauty and costliness, and don the gaberdine of disgrace; to drop the reins of the world's commerce which they held in their hands, and, instead, take a pack upon their back and wander from house to house, an object of ridicule and shame, and jeers and maltreatment. Think as they must have felt and thought and you will think less harshly of their feigned change of faith.

For a time all seemed bright. The "converts" were especially honored. They were appointed even to high ecclesiastical and municipal offices; their sons and daughters married into noble, and even royal families.

The few drops of baptismal water did not, however, change the character of the Jews. Their prosperity was as great as before, and, unlike the credulous and superstitious Spaniards, they failed to see any reason why they should lavish their wordly goods upon the Church. They preferred to do their own "taking care of," and their own "praying for" their soul. This was their crime. Their superior skill and industry, and the superior riches which these qualities secured, and their high standing in the community, aroused the priesthood's envy aud covetousness. Thus the charge arose that the converts had relapsed into their old faith.

The charge was not unfounded, The allegiance to the Church was that of compulsion, and it never was anything else, except a masked external allegiance. The heart, soul, conscience, mind, continued Jewish, and as fervently so as ever before. This "scandalous spectacle of apostates returning to wallow in the ancient mire of Judaism," was the pretext by means of which the Dominicans sounded the alarm. And the Inquisition came to cure them of their back-sliding.

Castile, the kingdom of Isabella, had till then refused admission to the Inquisition. At one time its introduction was recommended, and the whole populace arose in rebellion. Isabella herself trembled at the very mention of it. But in an evil hour *Thomas de Torquemada*, "condemned to infamous immortality by the signal part which he performed in the tragedy of the Inquisition, became her confessor. That man—if "man" I may name him—that vilest blot upon the history of religion, of Spain, of civilization, was the fiend incarnate. His very name still represents the superlative of maniacal fanaticism. He labored hard to infuse into the pure mind of the noble hearted Isabella a fanaticism as fiendish as was his. And still she recoiled from the thought of introducing the monstrous slaughtering institution in her domains. Torquemada brought the weight of the entire church to bear upon her conscience, and still she refused. The fiend was not yet baffled. He influenced her husband, the crafty and greedy Ferdinand of Aragon, to advocate his cause. The husband prevailed.

On the 2nd day of January, 1481, the Inquisition commenced operation in the city of Seville, with Thomas de Torquemada as Inquisitor General of Castile and Aragon A few years later it found its way into every prominent town of Spain, and confined itself everywhere almost wholly to the Jews. The severity, and savage alacrity of it, may best be learned from the appalling fact that during the eighteen years of Torquemada's ministry an average of more than 6,000 convicted

persons suffered annually from this cruel tribunal
by burning, or by condemnation to life long slavery,
or by endless torture, making an average of nearly seventeen a day, and the entire number punished during its existence in Spain, from 1481 to
1808, amounted to 340,000 persons.*

All this to protect the interests of religion. All
this for offenses so trivial that our blood boils
with indignation at the very thought of the heinous
cruelty. It was sufficient to burn a "convert," as a
relapsed heretic, upon the mere accusations of
crimes such as these: That he wore better clothes
or cleaner linen on the Jewish Sabbath than on other
days of the week; that he had no fire in his house
on the Jewish Sabbath; that he ate the meat of animals slaughtered by Jews; that he abstained from
eating pork; that he gave his child a Hebrew
name—and yet he was prohibited by law, under

---

*There is a Roman Catholic periodical entitled *La Bandera Catholica*
(The Catholic Banner) which is published in Barcelona, Spain; and on
July 29th, 1883, it published an article which caused one almost to think
he was living in the sixteenth instead of the nineteenth century
The writer of the article imagines the burning stake is a thing of the
near future. He says "Thank God, at last we have turned toward the times
when heretical doctrines were persecuted as they should be, and when
those who propagated them were punished with exemplary punishment
* * The establishment of the Holy Tribunal of the Inquisition must
soon take place Its reign will be more glorious and fruitful in results
than in the past, and the number of those who will be called to suffer
under it will exceed the number of the past. Our Catholic heart over
flows with faith and enthusiasm, and the immense joy which we experience
as we begin to reap the fruit of our present campaign exceeds all Imagination What a day of pleasure will that be for us when we see the
masons, spiritualists, free thinkers and anti-clericals writhe in the
flames, of the Inquisition!"

We also read in another article of the same Roman Catholic paper
that during the time of the existence of the Inquisition, from 1481 to 1808
in Spain alone there were 35,534 men and women burnt alive, and,
93,533 condemned to other punishments, because they differed in
opinion from the Romish Church

severe penalties, from giving a Christian name—
that on the Day of Atonement he had asked forgiveness; that he had laid his hands in blessing
upon his child's head, without the sign of the cross,
and numerous others, equally as harmless.   Most
of the charges did not even prove a relapse their
observance being, for the most, either purely acci-
dental or the result of early habit, or, what was
most frequently the case, pure invention   No
better chance existed for wreaking vengeance on
a Jew.   A simple accusation, even anonymously,
sufficed.   For the accused there was no safety
against malice; no facing the accuser, who perhaps, was his bitterest enemy; no trial; no cross
examination; no justice.   He was put under arrest
and conveyed to the secret chambers of the In
quisition, where, cut off from the world, he remained, sometimes for months, in complete ignorance of the nature of the charges preferred against
him.   Once there, the famous words of Dante
may be well applied to him: *"Lasciate ogni
speranze voich'entrate."* "All hope abandon, ye
who enter here."

At last he would be summoned before the Inquisitors and asked to confess.   And well for
him if he plead guilty.   It is true, he will be convicted, but he has escaped the tortures which are
well nigh beyond the power of endurance, and
which will soon force a confession, true or not true,
or which, even if endured, cannot save him, as he
will nevertheless be convicted on the strength of
positions of the accuser.

I shall spare you a recital of the tortures, of the sufferings endured in the deepest vaults of the Inquisition, where the cries of the victims could fall on no ear save that of the tormentors. It is difficult to realize that these iron-hearted and iron-handed henchmen, who thus eagerly, passionately, with a thirst for blood that knew no mercy, with zeal that never tired, devoted their whole life to cruelties such as we encounter here, could have been human beings, much less ministers of Christ. I shall spare you and spare myself a recital of these sufferings. I shall not speak of the tortures by rack and rope, and fire and water, how the victims' joints were dislocated, how every bone in their body was broken, how the body was roasted over a slow fire. I cannot speak of these tortures. I can only refer you to *"The History of The Inquisition,"* by Don Juan Antonio Llorento, whose records are authentic, as he himself was Secretary to the Inquisition; or to Mosheim's *"Ecclesiastical History,"* or to Prescott's *"Ferdinand* and *Isabella,"* volume I. chapter VII. To endure all these tortures, and live, was thought positive proof of Satanic life, and the strongest ground for burning. Nearly all plead guilty to whatever they were accused of, and to more, too, after a short experience with the rack. And confession brought public burning.

This was the last scene in the bloody tragedy, so wrongly named "Auto De Fe" ("Act of Faith"). It was a gala day for the town in which it was enacted. The proudest grandees of the land acted as escorts to the ecclesiastical henchmen. The roya party seldom missed this pompous ceremony, and not infrequently heaped fagots on the blazing fire with their own hands. A military escort led the unfortunate victims, clad in coarse yellow garments called "*san benitos*," garnished with a scarlet cross, and with hideous figures of devils and flames of fire. And a horrible appearance they presented, emaciated, lacerated, crippled, dazed by the light and fresh air which had been denied them for months.

The pyre is lighted. The flames shoot up. The victims writhe in agony.

Lo! a fierce wind arises. For a moment it blows the flames from the bodies. One of the victims speaks. It is Antonio Joseph, the Jewish celebrated author and classical dramatist of Portugal, where the performance of his dramatic pieces draws tears even to this day. Thus the venerable sage speaks:

"I own I belong to a faith which you yourselves acknowledge to be of Divine origin. God loved this religion, and He, according to my belief, is still attached to it, while you think He has ceased to be so; and because your belief differs from mine, you condemn those who are of the opinion that God continues to love what He formerly loved. You demand that we should become Christians, and yet you are far from being Christians yourselves. Be at least men, and act towards us as reasonable as if you had no religion at all to guide you and no revelation for your enlightenment." "*Osseitaro barbaro*" ("clip his beard"), some of the spectators shout, and im-

mediately one of the executioners besmears his
venerable beard, by means of a long brush, with
pitch and turpentine, and sets fire to it.   One
more cry, *"Sh'ma, Yisrael, Adonay Elahenu,
Adonay Echad"* ("Hear, O Israel, the Eternal,
Our God is One"), and the flames have done their
work, amidst the rapturous applause of the spectators, and amidst the pious ejaculations: "Blessed
be forever the goodness and mercy of the Holy
Inquisition.   Blessed be the Holy Trinity, the
sister of the Virgin Mary."   Not a tear among
the spectators.   Father, mother, husband, wife,
child, relatives, friends, all are eye-witnesses to
this bloody sacrifice, and yet from them not a sigh
of regret, nor dare they be absent, nor dare they
abstain from applauding, that would fasten sus-
picion upon them, and condemn them to a similar
fate.   A confiscation of the convicted possessions
ended the mournful tragedy.

Such was the clemency and generosity for
which Boabdil, the last of the Moorish kings, en-
treated.   Praised be God, now and forever, who
has emancipated us from the clemency and generosity of the Church.

Antonio Joseph da Silva.

————·o◇o·————

Auf dem Platze St. Domingo,
Vor der grossen Klosterkirche,
Harrt gespannt die wueste Menge,
Auf die Scheiterhaufen blickend.

Aus den Fenstern lugen Frauen
In den hellsten Festgewaendern,
Und es blitzen die Juwelen,
Um den Gottestag zu ehren.

Gilt es doch Antonio heute,
De sie ihren Plautus heissen,
Gilt es doch dem fruehern Liebling
Letzte Ehre zu erweisen.

Der beschuldigt eines Rueckfalls
In den alten Vaterglauben
Ihn will nun das Volk verlauegnen,
Ihn im Flammentode schauen.

Er, der sie mit seinem Spiele
Oft geruehlet und ergoetzet,
Heute wollen die Gemeinen,
An ihm selber ich ergoetzen.

Horch! schon toent die duestre Glocke,
Welche grauenvoll verkuendet,
Dass die Stunde war gekommen
Fuer den unbeugsamen Suender.

Alles gafft jetzt nach der Strasse,
Welche zu dem Platze fuehret
Und mit Schaekern und mit Spaessen
Sucht man sich die Zeit zu kuerzen?

Schau! da kommen sie die Schwarzen,
Die den Koenig stolz umgeben,
Schau! da kommen auch die Frevler,
Welche heute man verbrennet

Demuthsvoll ist ihre Haltung,
Und mit flehentlichen Mienen
Suchen sie wohl noch Erbarmen,
Ob sich nicht noch Mitleid finde?

Nur Antonio schreitet sicher
Und gefasst zur Richtestaette,
Ob er auch im Besserkleide
Und sein Antlitz abgehaermet

Nochmals wiederholt der Keonig
Zarte Worte an den Dichter,
Dass er noch in letzter Stunde
Seiner Seele Heil gewinne.

"Loes dich los von jenen Schaaren,
Die gekreuzigt den Erloeser,
Loes dich los von den Verstockten,
Deren Weg nur fuehrt zur Hoelle!"

"Wenn" entgegnet sanft Antonio
"Wenn" in Gottes Plan gelegen
Seines Sohnes Kreuzesleiden,
Um die Menschen zu erloesen.

Warum hasset ihr dann Jene,
Die den Gottesplan vollzogen?
Warum hasset ihr dann Jene,
Die gethan was Gott gewollet?"

Wohlgeneigt vernimmt der Koenig,
Wie der Dichter ihm erwidert,
Und es schien sein Herz zu ruehren,
Als er auf Antonio blickte.

"Deine Rede lass ich gelten
Und vergeben sei den Moerdern,
Doch, nun glaub' auch an den Meister,
Wolle dich uns zugesellen."

Aber unser Dichter wuerdigt
Nun den Koenig keiner Rede,

Da sich seine Seele ruestet,
Vor den Herrn der Welt zu treten.

Wuethend riss man von den Fingern
Ihm die Haut und dann die Naegel,
Still erduldet er die Qualen,
Lasst die Henker still gewaehren.

Eh' den Holzstoss er bestiegen,
Wendet er sich zu dem Volke,
Seinen Glauben zu verkuenden,
Zu lobinsgen seinem Gotte.

"Ew'ger Hort, dein Thun ist grade;
Recht sind alle deine Wege,
Dir allein will ich vertrauen,
Meine Seele dir empfehlen,

Du, vollkommen, ohne Zweiten,
Warst noch eh' die Welt erstanden,
Und in alle Ewigkeiten
Wird regieren nur dein Name!

Hoert mein letztes Wort, ihr Tauben,
Hor' es, Israel, mein theures;
Unser Gott, er ist der Ew'ge,
Unser Gott ist ewig. einzig!"

Wie empor die Flammen zuengeln,
Wie empor sie knisternd flackern,
Abzuwehren mit dem Tuche.
Sucht Antonio die Flammen.

Da taucht einer jener Henker,
In das Pechfass einen Besen,
Kreist ihn um den Bart Antonios
Fuer die gluehend muth'ge Rede.

Wie der Schrei die Luft durchzittert!
Wie jetzt selbst das Volk erbebet!
Schauer malet jedes Antlitz,
Dem noch eigen eine Seele.

Wer sind jene beiden Frauen.
Die verzweiflungsvoll sich krummen?

Ach, es ist Antonios Gattin!
Ach, es ist Antonios Mutter!

Die man teuflisch hat gezwungen,
Diesem Schauspiel beizuwohnen,
Ob vielleicht ihr Sinn sich aendre
Vor dem Zorngerichte Gottes?

Jetzt sieht man auch Maenner weinen,
Und beim Fortgeh'n sprach ein Alter:
"Wahrlich, der gleicht jenen Helden,
Die fuer ihren Glauben starben.

Ob man sie an's Kreuz geschlagen,
Oder ob man sie vergiftet,
Dieser Mann steht neben Jenen,
Die man feiert und verhimmelt."

Jener Bau der Glaubensrichter
Ist verschwunden von dem Boden
Lissabons und ein Theater
Hat die Staette sich erkoren.

Hoheitsvoll blickt auf Domingo
Dieser heitre Musentempel,
Der den Lorbeer ewig wahret
Allen, die gedient dem Schoenen!

CHAPTER XVI.

EXPULSION OF THE JEWS.

TORQUEMADA RESOLVES UPON IMMEDIATE EXPULSION OF ALL UNCONVERT
ED JEWS.—THE FATAL EDICT.—THE SPANIARDS MOVED TO PITY
—DON ISAAC ABARBANEL PLEADS WITH THF QUEEN.—
THE QUEEN HESITATES.—TORQUEMADA,THE FIEND,CONQUERS
AGAIN. —THE ILL-FATED JEWS SEEK AMONG THE DEAD
THE PITY WHICH THE LIVING REFUSE.
THE DEPARTURE.

With tearful eyes and bleeding heart we have
seen portrayed the mournful and tragic fate of
the Jews and Moors in Spain.   We were unwill-
ing eye-witnesses to sufferings and cruelties, which
we knew had never been equalled, and thought
could never be surpassed.   We thought we had
seen the climax of maniacal fanaticism   We
thought well might Thomas de Torquemada recline now beneath the laurels of infamous immortality he had won for himself, and henceforth
concentrate his frenzied zeal upon religious efforts,
less iron-hearted and less murderous.   We
thought now that Spain had completely van-
quished the Moor, had degraded the Jews, had
successfully taught the "convert" Jews a most
"burning" love for the Christian faith, by means of
the Inquisition's pitiless,slaughtering tribunal, now
that greed and bigotry and viciousness and

ambition had been satiated, we thought Ferdinand and Isabella would halt in their unpitying and unmerciful career, would pause long enough to gaze upon the terrible calamities they had inflicted upon the realm and upon innocent people, and would hasten to amend their ways, and repair their great wrongs.

It was natural for us to think so.   It is the experience of mankind that reaction accompanied by remorse, ever follows close upon the heels of rampant fury; that generosity and clemency, however fiercely the infuriated storms had lashed them into savage atrocity, will seek and find again their unruffled calm.   It is therefore we stand aghast at beholding the next brutish inhumanity of Torquemada.   Of a truth, he is not man but fiend, for to him principles which guide the actions of human beings are not applicable.   For him there exists no reaction and no remorse, no generosity and no clemency.   Where the most cruel of the cruel tremble at the mere thought, he executes sportively and in cold blood.   Where others rest their blood-reeking weapons in the belief that they have reached, at last, the summit of crime, he heartlessly advances as upon mere stepping stones to far greater cruelties to come.   He knew why he apprehended assassination now.   He knew why he secured an escort now of fifty horse and two hundred foot.   He was about to perpetrate a crime that should throw into the shade all that he had enacted hitherto.

The fate of the Moors had been decided.   The Inquisition thinned the ranks of the "convert" Jews.

The unconverted Jews, they that had preferred degradation to baptism; they that had preferred to take up their wretched abode as degraded out casts in the prescribed outskirts of the cities, to feigning adherence to a faith which their hearts hated; they that had sacrificed with singular resignation all that honest toil had honestly secured, and donned the garberdine of disgrace, and followed the degrading vocations enforced upon them by cruel laws, and suffered everywhere meekly unprovoked jeers, insult, outrage, assault, these must be dealt with now. Torquemada was resolved, and with him resolve was equal to execution, that in Spain the sun should shine upon none but pure Catholics, that the atmosphere of Spain should no longer be poluted by the presence of Jews; that none but "pious" Christians should tread upon its holy soil. He resolved upon expelling the Jews forever. They had long clogged the wheels of his triumphal car. He knew that there was a secret communion between "converted" and unconverted Jews. He knew that it was mainly due to their religious influence that the convert Jews relapsed again into Judaism. He knew that they provided spiritually and physically for the poverty-stricken and branded families of those of their race, whom the Inquisition burned, and whose possessions it confiscated. He knew that, despite rigorous measures and Dominican spies, converted and unconverted Jews met in subterranean caverns, and counseled and worshipped together, and comforted each other. He hit upon a cure at last. He knew a

remedy that would remove the clog forever.
He counselled immediate expulsion of all unconverted Jews.

In the year 1492, in the year in which Columbus discovered a new world, in the year in which
the Jewish sailor of Columbus' crew first set foot
upon the virgin soil of the western Hemisphere,*
strange fatality, in the same year that Spain opens
domains vast, destined to become the land of the
free, the blessed haven for the politically and racially
and religiously persecuted; in the same year, the
year 1492, she opens her portals at home, only to
thrust out, mercilessly, brutally, hundreds of
thousands of unoffending, industrious, intelligent
people, closes the gates behind them, and keeps
them barred nigh unto four hundred years.

On the 30th of March, 1492, the edict for the
expulsion of the Jews from Spain was signed by
the Spanish sovereigns at Granada. Torquemada
had triumphed. He had conquered the scruples
of king and queen and Grandees. The edict,
schemed and defended by him, had passed, and
the faithful execution thereof he took upon himself. Heralds proclaimed from the street corners of
every hamlet and village and city of Spain, that
all unconverted Jews, of whatever sex or age or condition, should depart from the realm before the expiration of four months, never to revisit it, on any

---

*The first Jew came to America with Christopher Columbus. His
name was Louis de Parres. He was one of the 120 companions of
Columbus, and the only one, who understood the Shemitic languages.
He and Rodrigo de Gerez were the first white men whom Columbus set
on shore. (See "Geschichte des Zeitalters der Entdeckungen von Prof
Sophus Ruge)

pretext whatever, under penalty of death, that all who should remain in the realm after the expiration of the four months would be put to death, as also all such Christian subjects, who should harbor, succor, or minister to the necessities of any Jew, after the expiration the term limited for his departure; that the Jews dispose in the meanwhile of their possessions as best they can, but are prohibited, under penalty of death, from having gold or silver in their possession at the time of their departure.

Unfortunate Jews! It was an idle hope when, seeing the sky lurid from the burning of your brethren upon the *quemaderos* (places of burning heretics), you thought that the cup of your afflictions was full at last. It was an idle hope, when, thinking of the invaluable services you rendered unto Spain, you thought her people could not possibly visit still greater calamities upon your innocent heads. Unfortunate Jews! Ye thought not of Torquemada, the fiend, when you fondly nursed these hopes.

When the edict was read from the corners of the streets and from the cross-roads, as the words that convey the sentence of death, strike terror in the heart of the condemned:

"So on the hearts of the people descended the words of the speaker.
Silent a moment they stood in speechless wonder, and then arose
Louder and ever louder a wail of sorrow and anguish." * *
—*Longfellow's "Evangeline."*

Maddening thought. Frenzied they rushed to and fro. Cries of terror and despair pierced the air. The Sierra Morena to the South, and the

Pyrenees to the North re-echoed the heart-rending wailing of the stricken ones.

Whither shall they flee? What country will dare offer them hospitable shores, when the greatest power in Europe thrusts them out helplessly, defencelessly, with a brand of infamy upon their brow?

Maddening thought, to go forth as exiles from the land of their birth, from their sweet domestic hearths, where they were wont to sit and tell of their long and proud and glorious past; to go forth from Spain, whose very soil seemed holy in their eyes; to leave Spain, that had been their fatherland for 1500 years, and more, long before the race of their present persecutors had heard of it, or had yet been civilized; to leave behind all that is near and dear to the human heart; the home of their proud achievements; the soil that held the graves of their own relatives and friends and of their illustrious sires, whose names had shed a brilliancy of light, that illuminated the darkness of their ages, and all the ages since; to leave Spain, whose very name was rapture to their souls; to leave it, never to return again; to leave home, possessions, friends, and go forth into the very jaws of death—on, ye Dominican fiends; slay them at once. If die they must, let them breathe their last upon the soil, which, next to Palestine, they worshipped most, but thrust them not out to perish in foreign lands.

Nay, we cannot conceive, to-day, the terror of this edict. Imagine, forbid it God—the very thought makes us shudder—imagine that an edict were suddenly to be issued that the 300,000 Jews of the United States—such was the number of the Jews of Spain—should be exiled from this country after the expiration of four months, never to return again; imagine such a calamity to befall us here, where our past is not yet a century old, and where the memories and associations of the past are not so deeply rooted as were those of Spain; imagine that we were told to go forth, branded with infamy, to cope, helplessly and defencelessly, and hopelessly with a hostile world; told to leave behind all that honest toil had gained for us; imagine that we had to assemble at the sea coast on a given day, to be packed into ships, like so many cattle, wives torn from husbands, babes from mothers, brothers from sisters, and then carried off, thousands of us to be hurled into the foaming deep, thousands to perish from want and exposure and cruelty, thousands to be disembarked upon uninhabited islands to be left a prey to wild beasts and starvation, thousands to be dropped on foreign shores, only to meet with still greater cruelties than were hitherto inflicted. Picture to yourself, if you can, miseries as terrible as these, happening unto us to-day, forbid it Heaven!—and even then will you only barely realize the calamity of this edict.

The sad fate which awaited the Jews touched the hearts of even the Spaniards. A delegation of them, including the most powerful grandees of the realm, waited upon the sovereigns, and implored them to revoke the terrible decree. Ferdinand and Isabella turned deaf ears to their en-

treaties. The great Don Isaac Abarbanel, the
last of the brilliant lights of the Jews in Spain, a
high officer in the service of Queen Isabella, threw
himself at her feet, and in heart-rending sobs he
burst forth:

"Ask for our life. and it is thine; ask for all our
possessions, they are thine, but if live we must,
then, Illustrious Queen, drive us not from off the
soil of Spain which is dearer to us than our life."

For a moment her inflexible will wavered,
another moment, and the mourning of 300,000
people might have been turned to rejoicing, and
the doom of Spain might have been averted, and
the history of Europe might have had a different
reading to-day. But that other moment was never
to come. Torquemada, who listened in an ad-
joining chamber to Abarbanel's tearful entreaty,
and to the queen's yielding words, rushed into the
royal presence, almost mad with fury, and point-
ing to the crucifix, he shrieked:

"Behold Him whom Judas Iscariot sold for
thirty pieces of silver ! Sell him now for a higher
price, and render an account of your bargain before God!"

The fiend had conquered again. The queen is
on her knees before him, imploring forgiveness
for her moment's weakness

A gloom pervaded the entire realm, as the time
of the departure drew hastily on. The Jews, attired in the deepest mourning, wandered restlessly about the streets. Peace dwelled no longer in
their homes. Their fountain of tears had run dry.
Their words became fewer, and more and more

painful. When children twined their little arms lovingly about their parents' neck, when pining husbands gazed upon their drooping wives, and in their mournful silence asked one another: A month hence, a fortnight hence, a week hence, to-morrow, where will father be? Where will mother be? What fate awaits husband, and what misery shall fall upon wife? What cruelty shall subdue brother, and to what life of infamy shall sister be sold? When upon such questions they brooded, and when did they not? madness seized upon them, and they rushed out to the burial places, and there, among the dead, they sought the pity and mercy and consolation the living could not give; there, in the graveyards, they lingered among the tombs of their dear departed, sometimes for three or four days in succession, not a morsel of food nor a drop of water passing their lips. And as they fixed their gaze upon the stately palms, that shaded them and the graves of their dead, with aching heart they lingered low·

> "More blest each palm that shades those plains
> Than Israel's scattered race;
> For, taking root, it there remains
> In solitary grace;
> It cannot quit its place of birth,
> It will not live in other earth.
> But we must wander witheringly
> In other lands to die;
> And where our fathers' ashes be,
> Our own may never lie."
>
> —*Byron's "Hebrew Melodies."*

Meanwhile the Spanish clergy was not idle. In the synagogues, in the public squares, in the open streets they preached the Love and Gentleness of the Redeemer, and appealed by argument, and by foul invectives, to the Jews, to accept the few drops of baptismal water, and remain in their adored native land. The Jews listened with a sullen indifference to these harangues. The suffering they endured for their faith convinced them more than ever of the absurdity of that religion which could inflict such cruelties. The treatment which the "convert" Jews received at the hands of their "Christian" brethren was surely not such as could inspire them with a burning desire for a change of faith. Rather exile, separation from fond home and fonder family, rather death than adopt a faith that fattened on blood and thrived on cruelty. "Let us remain firm," they cried to cheer on one another, "strong in our faith before our God, unyielding before our foes. We will live, if we are to live, if we are to die, we will die. Yet, living or dying, our covenant let us not desecrate; let our hearts never despair, let us never forsake, not even in the darkest hour, the living God of Israel." Noble sons and daughters of Israel. Ye sainted spirits of our departed ancestors of Spain, our hearts are filled with noble pride as we recount your heroic devotion to our God-given faith. In vain we turn the leaves of Historic record to find a parallel to your unswerving homage to conviction. Time can not diminish the lustre of your self-sacrificing deeds for the cause of Israel's truths. Four hundred years have silently emptied into the interminable Ocean of Time, and still Jew and Gentile, believer and unbeliever, all who worship at the shrine of political and racial and religious liberty, name you but to bless you, and are themselves inspired to virtue by their very breathing of your sainted names and heroic deeds.

At last the day for their departure arrived, August 2nd, 1492, the 9th day of *Ab. Tisha b'Ab*, 5252. The time had expired July 31, but they had implored for two days of grace, that this, their great calamity, might fall on *Tisha b'Ab*, the 9th of *Ab*, the annual day of fasting, the most calamitous day in the history of Israel.

It was on that day (586 B. C.) that *Nebukadnee-zar* laid the Temple of Solomon in ruins, and led the children of Israel from Palestine, as captives, to Babylon.

It was on that day (70 A. C.) that *Titus* destroyed the Second Temple, ended forever the political power and national life of Israel, and thrust the children of Israel from their native soil, the sacred soil of Palestine.

It was on that day (135 A. C.) that the fate of the *Barkochba* revolution was decided, and the last hope of Israel for political independence had vanished, and vanished forever.

And it was in the early morning of the same fatal day *Tisa b'Ab, 5252, August 2, 1492,* that the Jews of Spain repaired to their synagogues to worship there, for the last time, to sit upon the ground, with dust and ashes upon their heads, and girded with sack cloth, and read in accents sad, in accordance with an old established custom n Israel, Jeremiah's *"Lamentations"* over the destruction of the Temple, over the fall of Jerusalem and over the exile of the children of Israel into

Babylon. They had read the "Lamentations" before, they had read them year after year with tremulous lips, with accents fervent and deep, but they never knew their meaning before. That morning the broken heart spoke. And oh, what wails of sorrow, what sobs of contrition, what passionate out-breaks, as they repeated the verses:

"How does the city sit solitary, that was full of people. How is she become as a widow! she that was great among the nations. She weepeth sore in the night and her tears are on her cheeks, among all her friends she hath none to comfort her. Judah is gone into captivity because of affliction, she dwelleth among the nations, she findeth no rest. Her adversaries are powerful her enemies prosper, all that honored her despise her. It is nothing to you, all ye that pass by? Behold, and see if there be any sorrow like unto my sorrow, which is done unto me. Zion spreadeth forth her hands and there is none to comfort her. They cried unto them: Depart ye, ye are unclean, touch not, when they fled away and wandered, they said among the nations: they shall no more sojourn there. They hunt our steps, that we cannot go into our streets, our end is near, our days are fulfilled, for our end is come."

And forth they went from the house of God, the old and the young, the sick and the helpless virgin and youth, bride and groom, man, woman, child, with hearts bleeding, with steps tottering, with faces haggard and hollow and wan, with figure bent, and spirit broken as they gazed with a vacant stare for the last time upon their emptied homes upon the desolate scenes of childhood and youth.

On they went, overwhelmed yet speechless. But over them a chorus of martyr spirits, they that on that day perished, for their faith's sake, at the siege of Nebuchadnezzar, they on that day breathed their last for Israel's sake, at the siege of Titus, they that on that day had died with the death of Israel's hope, at the siege of Julius Severus, over the exiles of Spain, these martyr spirits chanted with doleful voices:

"Oh! weep for those that wept by Babel's stream,
Whose shrines are desolate, whose land a dream;
Weep for the harp of Judah's broken shell;
Mourn—where their God hath dwelt, the godless dwell!

And when shall Israel lave her bleeding feet?
And when shall Zion's songs again seem sweet?
And Judah's melody once more rejoice
The hearts that leaped before its heavenly voice?

Tribes of the wandering foot and weary breast,
How shall ye flee away and be at rest!
The wild dove hath her nest, the fox his cave,
Mankind their country— Israel but the grave "

Byron's "Hebrew Melodies."

TORQUEMADA.

Dunkle duestere Gestalten
Harren muerrisch vor dem Thore:
,,Heut erfolgt der Juden Auszug,
Heut ist der Termin verflossen!''11)

Boshaft wollen sie sich weiden
An dem Auszug der Verstoss'nen,
Und sie grinsen selbstzufrieden
Ob des Schicksals der Verstockten.

Einer ist's zumal, dess Grinsen
Teufelsbosheit von sich lodert,
Seine Blicke Schlangenblicke,
Sein Gebiss von Gift geschwollen;

Seine Worte Feuerschluende,
Sein Verlangen Tod und Moder,
Die Vernichtung seine Tritte,
Die Verwuestung sein Gefolge.

Wie sie zischeln die Gestalten,
Muerrisch harrend vor dem Thore.
,,Nur Geduld, Dominikaner!''
Ruft jetzt jener Hoellenbote.

,,Wie mein Name Torquemada,
Will ich weiter dafuer sorgen,
Dass die jetzt das Land verlassen,
Nicht entgehen sicherm Tode.

Fast war schon ihr Wunsch erfuellet,
Zu verbleiben unserm Boden,
Jener juedische Minister
Hatte Gold, viel Gold geboten.

Doch ich eilte zur Alhambra
Und das Crucifix erhoben,
Sprach ich zu dem Koenigspaare
Die entscheidend wucht'chen Worte:

Judas hat fuer dreissig Muenzen
Treulos den Herrn geopfert,
Und ihr wollet ihn verkaufen,
Arg geblendet von dem Golde?

Nun, so nehmt ihn und verkaufet
Euren Heiland, wie ihr wollet;
Hier ist er, o nehmt ihn gierig,
Wenn's euch duerstet nach dem Golde!

Diese Rede hat entschieden
Und ihr werdet heut die Horde
Aus dem Lande ziehen sehen,
Bald erscheinen sie am Thore.''—

Wie die drei Dominikaner
Harrt die Menge vor dem Thore.
Die in wilder Schadenfreude
Ob der Judensoehne spottet.

Torquemada naht der Masse
Und mit argen, list'gen Worten
Weiset er auf all' die Schaetze,
Die den Ausgewies'nen folgen.

Schelmisch weiss er sie zu hetzen
Gegen die verfehmten Opfer,
Und ertheilet mild den Ablass
Auf das Pluendern auf das Morden.

Welches Jubeln, welches Wimmern
Welches Pfeifen welches Trommeln
Dringt jetzt aus der Stadt herueber
Zu der Menge vor dem Thore!

Aber welcher Schauer fast uns
Bei dem Anblick dieses Volkes!
Sind es Schatten, sind es Geister,
Die an uns vorueberkommen?

Starren Blickes, gramvoll keuchend,
Ihren Ruecken tief gebogen,
Leichensteine ihre Lasten,
Moosbewachsen und geborsten.

Ach, es sind die einz'gen Schaetze,
Die den Elenden jetzt folgen,
Zum Gedaechtniss ihrer Ahnen,
Die da ruh'n in spanischem Boden.

Taeglich vor dem schweren Auszug
Weilten sie bei ihren Todten,
Weinten auf den theuren Graebern,
Ehe sie von dannen zogen.

Und sie zogen, wie die Lehrer
Gottergeben es geboten,
Dass nicht die Verzweiflung nahe.
Unter Pfeifen, unter Trommeln.

Ob auch viele wimmernd klagten,
Sang man doch zum Lobe Gottes
Und den tiefen Schmerz erdrueckend
Riefen sie das Sch'ma Israel!

Fast erschrocken von dem Anblick
Stand die Menge vor dem Thore,
Mitleid fuellte alle Herzen,
Und es schwand die Lust, zu morden.

Kaum gewahrte Torquemada
Judas wildgehetzte Sprossen,
Schaeumt er auf im Rachegeifer,
Und er grollt im finstern Zorne:

,,Koennt' ich baden in dem Blute
Der von Gott so lang Verworf'nen
Sollt' ich auch darin ertrinken,
Nichts verglich ich solcher Wonne!''

Also raset Torquemada
Und er sinket wie ein Todter
In den Arm der Ordensbrueder,
Die ein jaeher Schreck getroffen.

Judas Schaaren zieh'n vorueber
Unter Pfeifen unter Trommeln,
Allen Jammer uebertoenet;
,,Jubelt Voelker, unserm Gotte!''

Aus dem Fieberwahn erwachet
Torquemada und er tobet:
,,Seht ihr dort nicht die Gesellen,
Wie sie spannen ihren Bogen?

Wie sie nach dem Herzen zielen!
Helft! sie wollen mich erdrosseln,
Helft! sie wollen mich vergiften!
Ist das Einhorn nicht am Orte?12)''

,,Herr des Himmels, sei uns gnaedig!''
Rufen die Inquisitoren,
,,Unser Fuehrer ist von Sinnen,
Sein Verstand ist ihm genommen!''

Aus der Ferne immer leiser
Hoert man pfeifen, hoert man trommeln,
Jubeltoene dringen aufwaerts:
,,Jauchzet Voelker, unserm Gotte!''

CHAPTER XVII.

DISPERSION OF THE JEWS.

EXILES TRANSPORTED ON SHIPS—HEART-RENDING SCENES ON BOARD A
SHIP—SET ASHORE ON DESERTED ISLANDS TO STARVE—STARVING
JEWS GIVEN THE CHOICE BETWEEN DEATH AND CHRISTIANITY
MERCIFUL ITALY—CRAFTY PORTUGAL—TORQUEMADA'S
EDICT ECLIPSED—THE EXPULSION OF JEWS FROM
PORTUGAL—A CONDITION—THE KINGS' MARRIAGE
—CONTRACT—FINAL EXPULSION.

"The wild dove hath her nest, the fox his cave,
Mankind their country—Israel, but the grave."

Thus mournfully closed the last chapter. These
are sad words, fraught with anguish and
despair, yet however sad, however despondent
and hopeless, however much of grief, and anguish
and despair they convey, they befell the Jews of
Spain, and they fail altogether, when they are
asked to describe the sufferings and miseries
which met the unfortunate exiles, everywhere, in
their fruitless search for a quiet spot where they
might live or die in peace. Ships stood ready in
the harbors to carry nearly all of the banished
300,000 Jews whithersoever it suited the captains
best. Into these ships the exiles were literally
packed, crowded together without regard to sex

or age, often mother torn from child, husband from wife, brother from sister, friends from friends, and, separated on the coast meant separation for- ever.

' Words and the heart fail me to speak of the heart-rending cries of parent for child, and child for parent; of husband for wife and wife for hus- band; or of the wailing and lamenting, as Spain, the land of their birth, the home of their comfort and luxury and blessings, slowly faded out of sight and finally disappeared beneath the horizon.

And now begins a chapter in the history of Israel's suffering so frightful, so revolting that the pen and tongue recoil from dwelling upon it in detail. Before these sufferings, all that had been hitherto endured, faded into insignificance. And again it is avarice, and rapicity that bring these miseries upon them. The possession of the gold brought on their former sufferings, and now it is the want of it that opens their present miseries. Thou miserable gold! Whether ally or whether foe, ever thou wast the cause of Israel's untold sufferings! Because of thee, they had to purchase life, and because of thee they had to suffer death! The expulsion edict had prohibited the Jews, under penalty of death, from having money in their possession at their departure. And the Jews obeyed the mandate. What cared they for money when they could not enjoy it in their beloved Spain? What cared they for enjoyment, or even for life, when it was to be lived in distant and hostile lands? But the pirate captains and their heartless crews felt convinced, that the Jews

must have large sums of money sewed up in their
clothes, or concealed on their persons. No sooner
were they on high sea, when men and women and
children were ordered on deck, commanded to dis-
robe publicly, regardless of innocence of youth
and modesty of sex.   Many a virgin and
many a youth, many a husband and many a
wife dared to resist, not that they had money con-
concealed, but for shame sake, and the raging
billows rocked them into their eternal sleep for
their resistance. Disappointed in their search, their
thirst for gold was the more excited. Body after
body they ripped open,before the eyes of the unfortunate exiles, in the belief that they must have swallowed their gold and precious jewels. And disappointed in this, there followed a scene, a more detestable and dastardly one the sun never shone upon.
When the sailors had finally satiated their brutal
lusts upon the innocent and helpless, and faint from
terror and torture, and when the still surviving
victims had been made to cleanse the ships from
every trace of the blood of their friends and kin,
they were seized and dropped into the ocean
without a pang of conscience, and as unconcern-
edly as if the great God had created Jews for no
other purpose but to appease the beastly appetites of inhuman sailors, and serve as food for the
fishes of the sea.

And all this for the glory of Christianity! All
this in obedience to the teachings of the Church!
Heaven! Who can name the crimes that have been
perpetrated in Thy name? What seas of human
blood have been shed in the name of Christ, of
Mercy and Love and Peace and Good Will! The

Church had steeled the heart against every senti-
ment of pity and mercy. Feelings of compunction
of remorse in the perpetration of crimes against
the Jews, were taught to be the crime, and not
the crime itself. The tear of sympathy wrung
out by the sight of Jewish suffering was taught to
to be an offense to be expiated by humiliating
penance. Any one, it was taught, might con-
scientiously kill a Jew wherever he had an opportunity. The taste of blood, once gratified, begat
a cannible appetite in the people, and the more it
was satisfied the more intense became its thirst
for blood. Their zeal was not altogether unselfish;
every Jew accused of heresy, or killed, cancelled
—so the Church taught—for the accuser one hundred days from his future purgatory punishment.

Another captain was somewhat more merciful;
whether he had to expiate some of his tender-
heartness by humilating penance, ecclesiastical
history has neglected to record. He set all his
exiles on the shore upon a desert coast, leaving
the weak and the suffering pitilessly a prey to
wild beasts and to starvation. One of these
unfortunate deserted exiles who survived, tells us
how he saw his wife perish before his eyes, how
he himself fainted with exhaustion, and upon
awakening beheld his two children dead by his
side. For weeks, roots and grass furnished their
food. Each day brought fresh miseries and fresh
graves. These were days such as Shakespeare
speaks of:

"Each new moin——
New widows howl; new orphans cry; new sorrows
Strike heaven on the face "

Mothers, unable to bear the pining of their children, struck them dead, and then took their own life. Whole families folded themselves in loving embrace, and while thus embracing ended their life with their own hand. When the wild beasts came upon them, the exiles plunged into the sea, and stood shivering in the water for hours and hours, until the beasts retreated. Wearily they made their way onward, until, at last, they beheld the joyous sight of human settlements. Exhausted, they lay along the coasts, wasted by suffering and disease, and half demented from starvation. Down to the shore came the priests, and holding a crucifix in the one hand, and provisions in the other, the unfortunate Jews were given the choice between Christ and starvation. The flesh was stronger than the spirit. They begged for the bread, and ate at it ravenously, after the few drops of baptismal water had cleansed their soul from the foulest stains of infidelity. "Thus," says a pious Castilian historian, "thus the calamities of these poor blind creatures proved in the end an excellent remedy, that God made use of, to unseal their eyes, so that, renouncing their ancient heresies, they became faithful followers of the cross." How many hundred days of purgatory punishment were cancelled for this pious utterance of the Castilian, History again neglected to record.

Another ship load was cast out by a barbarous captain upon the African coast, where the African savages pounced down upon them, and abandoned themselves to frightful cruelties. The

men and youths they sold into slavery, the de-
fenseless women were brutally ravished; the
children at their mothers breasts, the aged and
the sick and the infirm were mutilated and tortured and murdered by the thousands.

Another ship load landed in the harbor of
Genoa. A graphic picture of their sufferings is
given by a Genoese historian, an eye witness of
the scenes, which he describes as follows:

"No one," says he, "could behold the sufferings
of the Jewish exiles unmoved. A great many
perished of hunger, especially those of tender
years. Mothers, with scarcely enough strength
to support themselves, carried their famished in-
fants in their arms, and died with them. Many
fell victims to the cold, others to intense thirst,
while the unaccustomed distress, incident to a sea
voyage, aggravated their maladies. I will not
enlarge on the cruelty and the avarice which they
frequently experienced from the masters of the
ships which transported them from Spain. Some
were murdered to gratify their cupidity, others
forced to sell their children for the expenses of
the passage. They arrived in Genoa in crowds,
but were not suffered to tarry there long, by reason of the ancient law, which interdicted the
Jewish traveler from a longer residence than
three days. They were allowed, however, to re-
fit their vessels and to recruit themselves for
some days from the fatigue of the voyage. One
might have taken them for spectres, so emaciated
were they, so cadaverous in their aspect, and
with eyes so sunken; they differed in nothing

from the dead, except in the power of motion, which, indeed, they scarcely retained. Many fainted and expired on the mole, which, being completely surrounded by the sea, was the only quarter vouchsafed to the wretched emigrants. The infection, bred by such a swarm of dead and dying persons, was not at once perceived; but when winter broke up, ulcers began to make their appearance, and the malady, which lurked for a long time in the city, broke out into the plague in the following year," *

More fortunate were the exiles that landed upon the shores of Naples. Its king, *Ferdinand I.,* was a prudent sovereign, a distinguished scholar, and, unlike the other rulers of Europe, he had succeeded in keeping his power above that of the Church, and his heart free from the inhumanity and bigotry of the clergy. He opened his kingdom to the Jews, made the great Abarbanel, formerly in the service of Isabella, of Castile, one of his cabinet officers, and personally defended the Jews from an attack of the clergy and of the populace, who held the presence of the Jews accountable for the plague which was then raging, as elsewhere in Europe, in Naples.

Equally as fortunate were those who landed upon the coasts where the Turks held dominion. Sultan *Bajazet* received them cheerfully, provided for them humanely, and directed their intellect and industry into useful channels. "Do they call this Ferdinand, of Spain, a prudent

---

*Piescott: "Feidinand and Isabella," Volume I, chapter xvii

prince," asks the Sultan, "who can thus impover-
ish his own kingdom and enrich ours?"

Nearly 150,000 souls made their way, by land,
to Portugal, whose king, *John II.*, dispensed with
his scruples of conscience so far as to allow his
greed to triumph over his creed. He granted
them a passage through his dominion on their way
to Africa, and the permission of an eight months'
stay in his realm, in consideration of a tax of eight
dollars a head, which immense sum he levied from
the native Portuguese Jews. Ferdinand and
Isabella threatened, and Torquemada incited the
Portuguese clergy, but *John II.* had over a million
of dollars to quicken his conscience and to wage
war if necessary, and expecting it, he instantly put
such of the Jewish exiles who were manufacturers
of arms and miners to work. But his clemency was
of short duration. It soon gave away to the most
frightful era of the exiles sufferings. When the news
reached the homeless exiles of the atrocious crimes
inflicted upon their brethren on their way to the
African coasts, by inhuman captains and heartless
crews, seeing nothing but cruel death before
them, whether going or whether remaining, they
preferred meeting death in Portugal, to exposing
themselves to the inhumanity and beastly lusts and
tortures of barbarous pirate sailors and African
savages, and listlessly awaiting death, and praying
for it, they remained after the time purchased for
their stay had passed away. To their misfortune
the plague broke out in Portugal and raged with
deathly fury. Immediately the church arose, held
the Jews responsible for the visitation of the plague,

and lashed the populace into a relentless fury, because of the visitation of the plague, and the breach
of contract on the part of the Jews.   The king's
creed awoke again simultaneously with the re-
awakening of his greed.   He issued an edict which
threw even that of Torquemada into the shade.
All Jewish children below fourteen years of age
were torn from their parents' arms, dragged into
the church, baptized; those under three years of
age were given to Christians, to receive a Christian
education, or in other words to be raised as slaves;
those between three and ten years of age, were put
on board of a ship and conveyed to the newly discovered, unwholesome island of St. Thomas, called
"*Ilhas perdidas*," "the isles of perdition," which
was colonized by Potuguese condemned crimnals,
to fare there as best they could.   Those between
ten and fourteen years were sold as slaves.   Then,
indeed, the cup of the their affliction was full to the
brim.   It was a stern truth which Lenau uttered,
when he said:

"Die Kirche weiss die Schmerzen zu verwalten
Das Herz bis in die Wurzel aufzuspalten."

The Jews have experienced fully the unequaled
skill of the Church in administering pain.   Mothers cast themselves at the feet of the tyrants and
pitifully begged to be taken with their babes;
they were heartlessly thrust aside.   Hundreds of
mothers mad with dispair, ran behind the ships
as they carried off the idols of their heart, and
perished in the waves.   The serene fortitude,
with which the exile people had borne so many

and such grievous calamities, gave way at last,and
was replaced by the wildest paroxysms of despair.
Piercing shrieks of anguish filled the land. Child-
less and broken-hearted they now sought to leave
the land, but they were told that they had for-
feited their right, and they were given the choice
between baptism and slavery. Thousands, after
enduring all they did, after leaving their beloved
Spain and all their wealth and ease, submitted to
baptism now, in the hope of being reunited with
their children. Thousands were sold as slaves,
yet prior to their being sold, they were submitted
to tortures, cruelties, outrages too revolting, too
repulsive, too heart-rending to be here narrated.

Terror seized upon the native Portuguese Jews,
when they helplessly beheld the cruelties to which
their Spanish brethren were subjected. They
knew they, themselves, could not escape the
wrath of the Church much longer, and they
thought of flight, and well had it been for them
had they made their escape then. While they
were making secret preparations, John II. died,
1495. He had been afflicted, on the very day
when the ships, laden with the Jewish exile children, set sail for the isle of the condemned crim-
inals, with a strange, painful malady, and had
lingered ever since.

His own promising son and successor preceded
him into the grave. His cousin *Manoel* ascended
the throne. He was the counterpart of his pre-
decessor, kind hearted, a promoter of learning,
eager to further the interests of his country by
discoveries abroad and by commerce at home.

Immediately he disfranchised the Jewish exiles sold into slavery, promised to recall the condemned children, and issued an edict, in which he commanded kind treatment to the Jews, and prohibited accusations against them. In their great joy the native Portuguese Jews sent an embassy to him, offering him large sums of money, voluntarily as a token of their gratitude. The king thanked them, reassured them of his good will, but refused to be paid for human kindness.

But, again had destiny decreed that a woman was to play an ignoble part in the tragic history of the Jews. A marriage was proposed between Manoel of Portugal, and the daughter of Ferdinand and Isabella, of Spain. Manoel was rejoiced with the proposal. Already he saw himself in the near future King of United Spain and Portugal, and of the entire New World. But Satan stepped between, dipped his pen in gall, and writing the marriage contract, demanded as one of the conditions, the immediate expulsion from Portugal of all the Jews, both natives and exiles.

The king hesitated. The fanatical daughter of fanatical parents persisted, argument made her more vehement. Torquemada might well be proud of his pupil—the possession of vast empires, and of the most powerful crown of Europe tempted, and the tempter conquered. He had purchased his right to the princess of Spain at a sacrifice of thousands and thousands of lives, and with the destruction of the very pillars of his nation's prosperity.

On the 30th of November, 1497, the marriage

contract was signed, and on the 20th of the following month appeared the edict of the expulsion
of the Jews from Portugal—The scenes of mourning and wailing and heartrending cries which resounded in Spain, re-echoed in Portugal, only the
more painfully, because of the terrible knowledge
they had since acquired of the meaning of the
word "Expulsion."

Manoel soon regretted his signing away his
most industrious, most intelligent and most prosperous citizens.   But the marriage contract held
him fast, and the Spanish queen kept a watchful
eye on him, and Torquemada upon both.   The
prospective vast empire, and the Spanish crown
still dazzled his eyes. He planned a strategy. He
thought he could force the parents to embrace
Christianity, and to remain, if he once succeeded
in getting all their children into his power, and
into the Christian faith.   He gave secret orders
for the repetition of the atrocious crime of having
all children under fourteen years of age seized
from their mothers' bosom and fathers' arm, dis-
persed through the kingdom to be baptised and
brought up as Christians.   The secret became
known.   Portugal again re-echoed the wails of
stricken ones.   Frantic mothers threw their children into deep wells or rivers.   Mothers were
known to take their babes from their breast and
tear them limb from limb, rather than to resign
them to Christians.   They would rather know the
bodies of their children in the grave, and their released spirit in Heaven, than have them adopt a
faith into which Satan sent his friends for their

schooling.   With all the parents' opposition the king's order was executed.   Many accepted baptism, but not enough to please the king, and to wreak vengeance upon them for thwarting his wishes, he revoked his edict, seized all who had not yet fled and sold them as slaves.

But Israel was not yet forsaken.   Italy, which had now become the seat of European learning, and had become very prosperous through the commercial and industrial zeal of the Spanish Jews, to whom it had offered refuge, and also Turkey, bade the Portuguese fugitives a hearty welcome.   What Spain and Portugal rejected, they knew how to value.   Even some of the Popes, Clement VII. and Paul III. (I rejoice to give them credit for it), favored their stay in Italy.   They had learned to appreciate the services of the Jews.   The flourishing Italian and Turkish Jewish congregations ransomed their brethren, and enabled them to settle in Ancona, Pesaro, Livorno, Naples, Venice, Ferrara and elsewhere, and the blessing of God rested upon whatever city the Jews were permitted to settle.

Many of the Portuguese Jews settled, and became prosperous, in the Indies, in Southern France and in Hamburg.   Others settled in the Netherlands, and became especially prosperons in Holland.   From Holland large numbers of the descendents of the Portuguese and Spanish exiles entered England, through the intercession of *Menasse ben Israel* with Oliver Cromwell, and from England and from the Indies and from Italy they entered the United States, into the land where tyranny is known no more, and persecution is fettered fast. Here dwell Christian and Jew side by side, peacefully, loving- ly, aiding each other, uniting with each other in the blessed work for which religion exists on earth, and in the spreading of the great principles of pol- itical and religious liberty. Here, where Christian extends the hand of fellowship unto Jew, and the heart of the Jew beats as loyally American as that of the Christian, solemnly they pledge:

'We swear to be a nation of true brothers,
Never to part in danger or in death,"
—*Schiller's "Tell"*

ISABEL LA CATOLICA,

In den Raumen der Alhambra
Wandelt Spaniens fromme Herrin
Isabella, die geruehmt wird
Als „katholische Regentin''.

Wandelt durch die Zauberhallen,
Die ein Maerchenglanz umspielet,
Und befriedigt laechelnd laesst sie
Auf den Thron sich langsam nieder.

Denkt voll Selbstgefuehl des Seufzers
Jenes letzten Maurenherschers:
„A Dios Granada!'' rief er,
„Ach, ich muss mich von dir wenden!''

Denket jenes alten Stammes,
Dem Vernichtung sie geschworen,
Jenes hartverstockten Stammes,
Den einst Gott in Lieb' erkoren.

Was sich zaehlte zu den Ketzern
Musste ihr Gebiet verlassen,
Die „katholische Regentin''
Laesst nur Einen Glauben walten.

Froelich schaut sie auf die Staette,
Wo Columbus einst gestanden,
Der ihr neues Land entdeckte,
Ihre Herrschaft zu entfalten.

Da erscheint vor ihr die Tochter,
Gleichfalls Isabel geheissen,
Die den Gatten den geliebten,
Still beklagt im Trauerkleide.

,,Sei willkommen mir zur Stunde!''
Sprach die Mutter froher Weise,
,,Eines Fuersten Liebeswerben
Hab ich heut dir mitzutheilen.

Portugals beruehmter Koenig
Legt sein Reichsland dir zu Fuessen,
Fuer ihn Spricht sein Ritterwesen,
Fuer ihn sprechen wicht'ge Gruende.''

Tief erschrocken hoert die Wittwe
Ihrer Mutter kurze Rede,
Deren Gruende, so betonet,
Stets im Rathschluss mussten gelten.

Isabella, unbeweglich,
Faehrt im gleichen Tone weiter:
,,Manoel muss mir geloben,
Alle Juden zu vertreiben.

Portugal und Spanien seien
Eines Sinnes, Eines Glaubens,
Toleranz ist unvertraeglich
Mit dem Einen, wahren Glauben.''

Diese Worte machen Eindruck
Auf die glaeubig fromme Wittwe,
Und zur Ehre Gottes will sie
Manoel in Lieb sich widmen.

Voller Eifer richtet selbst sie
An den Werber zarte Zeilen:
,,Soll ich dein Gebiet betreten,
Must die Juden du vertreiben.''

Manoel, der kluge Koenig,
Der mit Milde sonst regieret —
Isabellas Worte zuenden,
Keine Zeit will er verlieren.

Seine Liebe macht ihn grausam,
Unbesonnen folgt er Weibern,
Ja, noch ueberbieten will er
Sie, wenn's geht, an Grausamkeiten.

Den Befehl erlaesst er schleunig,
Dass bis zu bestimmtem Tage
Die Bekenner des „Allein'gen"
Alle sein Gebiet verlassen

Alle Kinder die der Jahre vierzehn
Noch nicht zaehlen, soll man geben
Frommen Cristen zur Erziehung,
Dass sie fromme Christen werden.

Vor dem Jammerschrei der Muetter
Sucht sich Manoel zu retten,
Blickend auf das zarte Bildniss,
Gleichend einem holden Engel.

Isabella laesst vergessen
All das Leid, das er veruebet,
Und mit Liebesgluthen eilt er,
Seine Gattin heimzufuehren.

Schon das Hochzeitsfest ist truebe,
Ploetzlich starb der Kronprinz Spaniens
Und mit Trauer im Gemuethe
Zieh'n nach Evora die Gatten.

Manoel, dir drohet mehr noch:
Eh' ein kurzes Jahr entschwindet
Wirst du deine heissgeliebte
Isabel als Leiche finden.

Tief bewegt steht vor der Bahre
Portugals beruehmter Koenig,
Ihn erschreckt das Schrei'n des Kindes,
Das ihm Isabel geschenket.

Ob er jetzt wohl hoert das Schreien
Jener Muetter, angsterfuellet?
Das Geschrei der armen Kinder,
Denen man geraubt die Muetter?!

Tiefgebeugt steht vor der Bahre
Isabella, „die Katholische",
Bruetend, sinnend, bleichen Blickes,
Findet sie jetzt keine Worte.

Aus dem Trauerkreise zieht sie
Nach Granada mit dem Kinde,
Das in ihrem herben Schmerze
Ihr als einziger Trost geblieben.

In den Raeumen der Alhambra
Wandelt Spaniens fromme Herrin
Isabella, die geruehmt wird
Als „katholische Regentin".

Wandelt durch die Zauberhallen,
Die ein Maerchenglanz umspielet.
Und mit kummervollem Herzen
Laesst sie auf den Thron sich nieder.

Denket da des schweren Leides,
Dass sie Schlag auf Schlag betroffen,
Und es loesen sich die Seufzer.
Weinend sitzt sie auf dem Throne.

Einz'ger Sohn, des Thrones Erbe,
Musst' so frueh ich dich verlieren,
Isabella, liebste Tochter,
Musst' so frueh ich dich verlieren!

Ach, Maria, meine Tochter,
Musst' so frueh ich dich verlieren,
Einsam wandelt Katharina,
Die vom Manne sich geschieden.

Meine Leiden mehrt Johanna,
Aermstes meiner guten Kinder.
Ihres Gatten treulos Treiben
Hat ihr den Verstand verwirret".

Also seufzet Isabella,
Seufzet auf dem stolzen Throne,
Da erscheint vor ihr ein Diener,
Doch er zoegert mit dem Worte.

Boeses ahnend ruft die Koenigin:
„Welches Unglueck wirst du melden?
Sprich nur, ohne mich zu schonen,
Haertres kann mich nicht mehr treffen".

„Don Miguel, das herz'ge Soehnchen,
Den in Ihrer grossen Liebe
Ihre Majestaet als Kronprinz nannten,
Eben ist er sanft verschieden"

Lautlos hoert es Isabella,
Die fuer Gott nur stets gehandelt
Und mit frommer Duldermiene
Schleicht sie wankend aus dem Saale.

CHAPTER XVIII.

EFFECT OF THE EXPULSION.

A Brief Review.—-Curse of God Visited Upon Spain.—The church
A False Prophet.—With Expulsion of the Jews and Moors
Spanish Prosperity Ceases.—Spaniards Experience Some
of the Sufferings Which the Jews and Moors had
Endured.—Spain Makes Amends.—The Moors
Lost.--The Jews Live.

A few words more and our task is ended. A
few words more and we shall bid a last farewell
to unfortunate Spain, once so sunny, so prosperous,
so intellectual, and so fair. A few words more
and our goodly vessel, staunch and strong, will
furl its eager wings and speed us straight across
the foaming deep, and land us once again upon
Columbia's heaven blessed and freedom-kissed
virgin soil. As we predicted, so it came to pass.
Our journey back into the centuries of the past,
and into foreign lands. and among foreign peo-
ples, has proven a profitable one, and as mem-
orable as profitable. Events and scenes, beautiful and loathsome, joyous and tearful, soul refreshing and execrable, followed each other in rapid
succession. There was much, which, despite the
most authentic historic sources, seemed fabulous,

incredible, impossible.   Men and women and the
states of society and civilization in which they
lived and played their parts, were described,
which startled us for their peerless magnificence,
for their marvelous intellectuality, scarce equalled
even now, and led us to suppose that we were not
dealing with facts, but with the imagination of some
rich phantasy. And events and achievements were
recounted which struck terror into our very soul,
and caused the heart to rise in rebellion against
the mind when it was asked to believe them as
actual occurrences, and not as some distressing and
revolting and blood-stained work of fiction. And
yet all that was told, and all that was described,
and all that was recounted was history, and true
history, strange and incredible, marvelous and
anomalous though it did appear.

Two races of men engaged our attention most,
the Jews and the Moors. When first we met
the Jews in the southwestern corner of Europe, we
found them a prosperous community, large in
numbers, loved and appreciated by their heathen
neighbors, busily engaged in transforming Spain into a granery and into the garden spot of Europe,
and contributing largely, by their high morality and
intelligence, by their skill and industry to the nation's prosperity.

With the advent of the power of Christianity in
Spain, in the Sixth Century, a sad change took
place. It marked the beginning of the martyrology
of the Jews in Europe. Thousands were massacred, thousands were dragged to the baptismal
font, thousands were forced to take the staff of

exile. But not for long. A deliverer arose from the Arabian peninsula and hastened to their rescue. This Arabian people, agile in the use of arms, dexterous in the training of horses, capable of sustaining great fatigue and hardship, and, true to the Semitic race, intellectual and sagacious, had lived till late in the Sixth Century a peaceful, nomadic life. Suddenly they were awakened out of their religious and political inactivity by their great leader Mohammed, the prophet. He kindled in their hearts the fire of enthusiasm, and led them forth to establish throughout the world his faith and his dominion. Asia submitted, Africa submitted. The early dawn of the Eighth Century saw them, where the African continent protrudes boldly to meet the continent of Europe, casting wistful glances across the straits of Hercules, upon Andalusia's beauteous lands. The exiled Jews and Christans, roused to rebellion by the religous and political tyranny of Spain, conspired with the Mohammedan invaders, and the portals of Spain were opened to the people of Arabia, and Europe to the creed of Mohammed. The exiled Jews returned to their country, and the baptized to their cherished faith, for the Arab-Moors tolerated both the Hebrew people and their faith. Moorish and Jewish skill and industry and intelligence united, and united they became—and they maintained that distinction for many centuries—the most prosperous and most intellectual people of Europe, at a time when the rest of Europe was numbed into a death-like torpor, mentally spell-bound, industrially entranced,

politically enslaved, morally degraded and religiously fettered, by a corrupt priestcraft, to ignorance and superstition.

Eight centuries long Jew and Moor toiled side
by side, and during all these centuries, the Jews,
with some few exceptions, politically tolerated,
and religiously free, arose to great wealth and
commercial importance, clothed honorably high
political offices, and occupied a social and intellectual position never equalled in Europe before
or since.

But the Mohammedan power began to wane, and
with its waning came the terrible change in the
fortunes of the Hebrew people. With Moorish
decline awakened the eagerness of the Spaniards
for the provinces from which the Arabian invaders
had driven them, and with it grew a most fanatical zeal for the expulsion from its territories of
every belief save that of Christianity.

A desperate struggle ensued. Province after
province the Moor was forced to yield to the relentless foe. At last all was lost. The Mohammedan power in Spain was crushed. The Moors and
Jews were given the choice between baptism and
expulsion. Hundreds of thousands of them
feigned allegiance to the Church of Christ, and
remained. Hundreds of thousands of them, true
to their faith, parted heart-broken from the land
that was dearer to them than their own life. The
remaining baptized Jews and Moors were soon
suspected of relapsing into their old faith, and the
Inquisition was brought and burned them by the
thousands, and thinned the ranks of the exile Jews.

By far the greater number perished from cruelty, exposure, starvation, disease, in their search for a quiet spot where they might live or die in peace. Wherever the remainder of them was permitted to settle, thither they brought blessings *** verifying the promise of God: "They that bless thee will be blest.*

And so, too, was verified the other half of that promise: "They that curse thee will be cursed." The curse of God has hung heavily upon Spain, ever since she had dared to lay violent hand upon God's anointed, ever since she cruelly massacred, burned and exiled the most thrifty, the most industrious, the most intellectual people that ever trod her soil, and made her the glory of Europe and the pride of the world. For a short time only, lingered her prosperity after the expulsion of the people that had created that prosperity. The New World, the discovery of which the Jews and Moors had made possible, poured into the mother country a prodigious wealth, which hastened the ruin of Spain. It intoxicated the Spaniards, and when the sobering came, the effect was terrible. Had they had the skillful, and industrious and intelligent Jews and Moors to turn the vast treasures, which poured into Spain with every vessel, into useful channels, Spain would have maintained her position as leader in the commercial world, and Italy, and France, and the Netherlands, the new homes of the Jews, would never have seized it from her, and Spain would

*Cf. Lecky's "Rationalism in Europe" vol i. chap. vi.
**Genesis xii: 3.

not have been to-day what she is. But, instead,
it flowed into the coffers of the greedy and insatiable Church, and the richer the Church became the more terrible became its tyranny, and
the greater the inducement for laymen to enter
it. Convents and Churches multiplied with such
vast speed, that early in the Seventeenth Century
the Spanish historian enumerates upwards of
9,000 monasteries, besides nunneries, 32,000
Dominican and Franciscan friars, 14,000 chaplains
in the diocese of Seville, and 18,000 in the diocese
of Calahorra.

The State was completely in its power. Even
Charles V and Phillip II, sovereigns not to be
matched in any other country for a period of equal
length, submitted cheerfully to the power of the
Church, and thought it a blessed privilege to do
so. It was Charles V's great boast that he always preferred his creed to his country, and proved his boast by slaying in cold blood, in the Netherlands, over 50,000 peaceful, industrious, good
Christian citizens for their religious opinions. The
cannibal appetite of the Church had to be appeas-
ed, when the stock of Jewish and Moorish victims
was exhausted, truth and knowledge-seeking
Christians had to supply their places upon the
quemaderos, and in the torture-dungeons of the
Inquisition. Even with his last breath he commanded his son, Philip, never to show favor to
heretics, to kill them all, to uphold the Inquisition
as the best means for the establishment of the
true belief. Philip II. proved himself worthy of
his sire. He has written his services to the Church

upon history's records with flames of fire and letters of blood.

With amazing swiftess Spain's once invincible
power began to disappear, becoming weaker with
every century, and to-day the population of more
than 30,000,000 of people before the expulsion of
the Jews and Moors has dwindled down to about
one half of that number, while her neigboring
countries have increased in numbers and prosperity. "So rapid was the fall of Spain," says Buckle
in his "History of the Civilization of England,"
Vol. II, Chap. I, "that the most powerful monarchy existing in the world was depressed to the
lowest point of debasement, was insulted with
impunity by foreign nations, was reduced more
than once to bankruptcy, was stripped of her fairest possessions, was held up to public opprobrium,
was made a theme on which schoolboys and mor-
alists loved to declaim, respecting the uncertainty of human affairs. Truly did she drink to
the dregs the cup of her own shame. Her glory
had departed from her, she was smitten down and
humbled. The mistress of the world was gone;
her power was gone, no more to return.

The Church had proven itself a false prophet.
"Once purge blessed Spain," it preached to its
credulous followers, "of the presence of the accursed Jews and Moors, and yourselves and your
families will be under the immediate protection
of Heaven. The earth will bear more fruit. A
new era will be inaugurated, Spain will be at ease.
People will live in safety, and gather in peace and
in abundance the fruits of their handiwork."

Such was the prophecy: but bitter its fulfilment. With the expulsion of the Jews and Moors large bodies of industrious and expert agriculturists and skilled mechanics were suddenly withdrawn, and there was no one to fill their place. The cultivation of rice, cotton and sugar, and the manufacture of silk and paper was destroyed at a blow, and most of it was destroyed forever, for the Spanish Christians, still intoxicated with their military and financial and social greatness, considered such pursuits beneath their dignity. To fight for the king and to enter the Church was honorable, but everything else was mean and sordid. Whole districts were deserted and have never been repeopled to the present day. The brigands soon occupied the places formerly so beneficially filled by honest toilers. In less than fifty years 16,000 looms of Seville, giving employment to 130,000 persons, had dwindled away to less than 300, and its population to one quarter of its former number. The mines stood idle until foreigners took pity of some of them. The others are idle still. A little over one hundred years ago the Spanish government being determined to have a navy, found it necessary to send to England for shipwrights; and they were obliged to apply to the same quarter for persons who could make ropes and canvas, the skill of the natives being unequal to such arduous achievements; and early in the eighteenth century they were obliged to import laborers from Holland to teach the Spaniards the art of making wool, an art for which in their glorious past they were especially famous.

The consequences of this industrial and agri-
culturial standstill could not fail. Famine set in.
The grandees murmered aloud against the State
for expelling the Jews and Moors. The citizens
of Madrid fell down in the streets famished and
perished where they fell—so had famished and
died the Jewish exiles—anarchy prevailed.
Peaceful citizens organized themselves into bands
and going in search of bread, broke open private
houses, and robbed and murdered the inhabitants
in the face of day—thus had been murdered the
Jewish exiles. Verily God's prophecy was fulfilled: "And I will bless them that bless thee, and
curse them that curse thee, in thee shall the families
of the earth be blessed."*

Spain's intellectual decline kept steady pace with
its political and industrial decay. No more is she
the center of Europe's learning. No more does her
intellect shed luminous rays all over the world.
The Moor and the Jew have fled her provinces,
and darkness covers her lands, the shadows of
night again brood stiflingly over her people.
Her poverty has made her ignorant, her ignorance has made her intensely fanatic, and her
fanaticism is, to this day, the enemy of all social
and intellectual advance. For two centuries and
more investigation likely to stimulate thought
was positively prohibited. In the measure that
her sister countries advanced intellectually she
declined, and in proportion as they shook off the
fetters of the Church, she cheerfully submitted to
have them drawn tighter about her. Until the

*Gen xii:3.

eighteenth century Madrid did not possess a single public library, and to-day the number of volumes in all the Spanish libraries cannot reach 500,000. The library of Cordova in the tenth century, before the printing press was discovered, counted over 600,000 volumes. The Government library of Paris and that of London count respectively over 1,500,000 and over 2,000,000 volumes. So late as the year 1771 the Unversity of Salamanca, the most ancient and most famous seat of learning in Spain, publicly refused to allow the discoveries of Newton to be taught, and assigned as a reason that his system was not consonant with revealed religion. Buckle quotes from Spanish sources, an epistle which will illustrate the abysses of ignorance into which the Spanish intellect had sunk. About a century ago some bold men proposed that the streets of Madrid should be cleansed. The proposal was met with excited indignation. The question was submitted by the government to the medical profession. They reported unfavorably. They had no doubt that the dirt ought to remain. To remove it was a new experiment, and of new experiments it was impossible to foresee the issue. Their fathers having lived in it, why should they not do the same? Their fathers were wise men, and must have had good reasons for their conduct. The filth shall remain. And it did remain. And it did make Spain the, alas, too frequent victim of plague and cholera, and we now no longer wonder that a year ago, when the cholera raged in Spain, the people arose against the physicians for being asked to resort to medicines and cleanliness and not to Relics and Holy Water.

Intellectually Spain sleeps on, dreams on, receiving no impressions from the rest of the world and making none upon it. "There she lies," says the historian, "at the further extremity of the continent, a huge and torpid mass, the sole representation now remaining of the feelings and knowledge of the middle ages. And what is the worst symptom of all, she is satisfied with her own condition. Though she is the most backward country in Europe, she believes herself foremost. She is proud of everything of which she should be ashamed. She is proud of the antiquity of her opinions; proud of her orthodoxy; proud of the strength of her faith; proud of her immeasurble and childish credulity; proud of her unwillingness to amend either her creed or her customs; proud of her hatred of heretics, and proud of the undying vigilance with which she has baffled their efforts to obtain a full and legal establishment on her soil."

But since Buckle penned these forcible lines, she has made a change. She has recalled the Jews, some five years ago, after 400 years of banishment. Her eyes have been opened at last, and she now seeks to repair her wrongs to the people she afflicted most. And prosperity will follow the re-entrance of the Jews. Spain will again be blest; it may take time, church tyranny will first have to be crushed and ignorance and superstition rooted out, but crushed and rooted out they will be. Her harbors on the Alantic and Mediterranean will again command the com-

merce of both hemispheres. Her cities will
again teem with people. Her towns will
again flourish, her manufactures will again be
skillful, the produce of her exuberant soil will
again gladden the heart of mankind. Her inexhaustible mines, rich in all the precious and all
the useful metals, her quarries of marbles and her
beds of coal will again set the wheel of industry
into busy motion. She will be blest again. She
must be blest again, for such is the word of God.
She has held out the hand of friendship to His
anointed people, and they that bless them will be
blest.

The Moors, Spain no more can recall. The
Arab-Moors, such as they were in Spain, exist no
longer. Their descendents roam as benighted
Bedouins over those regions of Africa which their
ancestors once illumined by the light of learning.
Gone is most of their literature The beautiful
accents of the classic Arabic tongue are heard
no more. Darkness, deep darkness, rules
over the Arabian peninsula now. The history
that their sires in Spain have made our civilization their debtor, reads indeed, to-day, like unto
a fairy tale.

But the Jews live, and fulfill the glorious mission for which they have been scattered throughout the world. The people chosen by the Eternal
Jehovah to be His priest people cannot die. The
people that has seen the tidal waves of Babylon,
Persia. Greece, Egypt, Rome roll over it and instead of engulfing it has lived to see them en-
gulfed; the people that live after a thousand strug-

gles, after deeds of heroic courage that Rome, and Athens, and Sparta, and Carthage have never equaled, outliving them all; the people that still lives, after eighteen centuries of persecution, and still is united, though scattered the wide world over, and though not held together by the ties of any fatherland, was never destined to be annihilated by any Church or by any race of men. The Jew is older than both, and will outlive them both. Time and death wield no power over him. Emerson spoke truly:

> "This is he who, felled by foes,
> Sprung harmless up, refreshed by blows:
> He to captivity was sold,
> But him no prison bars would hold;
> Though they sealed him in a rock,
> Mountain chains he can unlock;
> Thrown to lions for their meat,
> The crouching lion kissed his feet;
> Bound to the stake, no flames appalled,
> But arched o'er him an honoring vault."

Such is the Jew. He is as indestructible as his religion, and as eternal as his God.

FAREWELL TO SPAIN.

————••o◆o••————

Schoenes Land der Jugend Traeume!
Habe endlich dich durchzogen,
Ueberall nur Freude findend,
Herzlich war ich aufgenommen.

Schoen bist du und lachend woelbt sich
Ueber dir der blaue Himmel,
Dich umrauschen Meereswellen
Und dir ragen Bergesgipfel.

Auf den Feldern blueht der Weinstock,
Feigenbaeume decken Huetten,
Purpurn glaenzen die Granaten,
Und der Oelbaum strotzt in Fuelle.

Allzeit duften dir die Rosen
Und die Myrthen in dem Garten,
Gleich Orangen und Citronen
Bilden Waelder dir die Palmen.

Schoenes Land, das frohen Menschen
Steigert den Gesang zum Jauchzen,
Land des Weines und der Taenze
Und der anmuthsvollen Frauen.

Land der Dichter und der Ritter,
Und der muntren Volkessitten,
Land fuer Hohes sich begeisternd,
Und gefuehrt vom Edelsinne.

Einst, ja einst, da sangen mit euch,
Judas Soehne, euch zum Ruhme
Waren eng mit euch vereinet,
Gleicher Sinn hat euch verbunden.

Sie auch stellten manchen Denker,
Der noch heut' im Volke lebet,
Und ihr habt von eurem Namen
Vieles ihnen zu verdanken.

Sie auch stellten manchen Dichter,
Der in urer schoenen Sprachen
Liedere sang in allen Toenen,
Wie sie nur Iberien athmet.

Trefflich waret ihr gebildet,
Die Natur hat euch geschmuecket.
Doch, es waren boese Maechte,
Die euch falsche Wege fuehrten.

Jene boesen Maechte sind es,
Die euch das Verderben brachten,
Despotismus war die eine,
Fanatismus war die andre.

Schon in diesen wen'gen Blaettern
Hoert ihr eine Welt von Jammer.
Rastlos jagten schwarze Wolken,
Euren Himmel zu umnachten.

Doch es nahen nach den Stuermen
Endlich jene lichten Zeichen,
Die die neue Zeit verkuenden,
Alte Schaeden auszugleichen!

Ja, sie nahen, jene Geister,
Fuer die Wahrheit sich zu muchen;
Ja, sie nahen, jene Maenner,
Die fuer Menschenrecht ergluehen.

D'rum sei alles Leid vergessen,
Bruedern ziemt es, zu vergeben,
Ob der grossen Geisteswerke
Wollen freudig wir vergeben.

Ob der grossen Geisteswerke,
Die wir danken euren Gassen,
Unserer Geschichte Glanzpunkt,
Seit wir Judas Land verlassen.

Moege eure Kraft sich sammeln,
Wohlstand eure Wege schmuecken,
Wissenschaft und Kunst erstarken
Frieden euer Land begluecken.

NOTE.—The German Poems, at the end of Chapters XV., XVI.
XVII., XVIII., are selections from Dr. M. Levins' ''Iberia ''

Note 12, page 205, alludes to the fact that Torquemada was in con
stant dread of assassination, and that he always carried the horn of a
unicorn with him, believing that it would save him.

The poetic selections on pages 133, 134, 135, are from the writings
of Gabirol. Ha Levi is the author of the first selection, and Moses ben
Ezra of the second selection on page 136.

INDEX.

———

Made in the USA
Middletown, DE
03 February 2021